D0389231

The Death Penalty

OPPOSING VIEWPOINTS®

Other Books of Related Interest

Opposing Viewpoints Series

America's Prisons
Crime and Criminals
Criminal Justice
The Legal System
Opposing Viewpoints in Social Issues
Problems of Death

Current Controversies Series

Capital Punishment
Crime
Guns and Violence
Hate Crimes
Prisons
Youth Violence

At Issue Series

Does Capital Punishment Deter Crime?
Guns and Crime
How Should Prisons Treat Inmates?
School Shootings
What Is a Hate Crime?

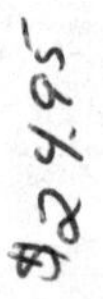

The Death Penalty

OPPOSING VIEWPOINTS®

Mary E. Williams, *Book Editor*

Daniel Leone, *Publisher*
Bonnie Szumski, *Editorial Director*
Scott Barbour, *Managing Editor*

Greenhaven Press, Inc., San Diego, California

Cover photo: California Department of Corrections

Library of Congress Cataloging-in-Publication Data

The death penalty / Mary E. Williams, book editor.
p. cm. — (Opposing viewpoints series)
Includes bibliographical references and index.
ISBN 0-7377-0791-7 (pbk. : alk. paper) —
ISBN 0-7377-0792-5 (lib. : alk. paper)
1. Capital punishment. I. Williams, Mary E., 1960–
II. Opposing viewpoints series (Unnumbered).

HV8694 .D3824 2002
364.66—dc21 2001040456
CIP

Printed in the U.S.A.

Greenhaven Press, Inc., P.O. Box 289009
San Diego, CA 92198-9009

> "Congress shall make no law. . . abridging the freedom of speech, or of the press."
>
> *First Amendment to the U.S. Constitution*

The basic foundation of our democracy is the First Amendment guarantee of freedom of expression. The Opposing Viewpoints Series is dedicated to the concept of this basic freedom and the idea that it is more important to practice it than to enshrine it.

Contents

Why Consider Opposing Viewpoints?

"The only way in which a human being can make some approach to knowing the whole of a subject is by hearing what can be said about it by persons of every variety of opinion and studying all modes in which it can be looked at by every character of mind. No wise man ever acquired his wisdom in any mode but this."

John Stuart Mill

In our media-intensive culture it is not difficult to find differing opinions. Thousands of newspapers and magazines and dozens of radio and television talk shows resound with differing points of view. The difficulty lies in deciding which opinion to agree with and which "experts" seem the most credible. The more inundated we become with differing opinions and claims, the more essential it is to hone critical reading and thinking skills to evaluate these ideas. Opposing Viewpoints books address this problem directly by presenting stimulating debates that can be used to enhance and teach these skills. The varied opinions contained in each book examine many different aspects of a single issue. While examining these conveniently edited opposing views, readers can develop critical thinking skills such as the ability to compare and contrast authors' credibility, facts, argumentation styles, use of persuasive techniques, and other stylistic tools. In short, the Opposing Viewpoints Series is an ideal way to attain the higher-level thinking and reading skills so essential in a culture of diverse and contradictory opinions.

In addition to providing a tool for critical thinking, Opposing Viewpoints books challenge readers to question their own strongly held opinions and assumptions. Most people form their opinions on the basis of upbringing, peer pressure, and personal, cultural, or professional bias. By reading carefully balanced opposing views, readers must directly confront new ideas as well as the opinions of those with whom they disagree. This is not to simplistically argue that everyone who reads opposing views will—or should—change his or her opinion. Instead, the series enhances readers' understanding of their own views by encouraging confrontation with opposing ideas. Careful examination of others' views can lead to the readers' understanding of the logical inconsistencies in their own opinions, perspective on why they hold an opinion, and the consideration of the possibility that their opinion requires further evaluation.

Evaluating Other Opinions

To ensure that this type of examination occurs, Opposing Viewpoints books present all types of opinions. Prominent spokespeople on different sides of each issue as well as well-known professionals from many disciplines challenge the reader. An additional goal of the series is to provide a forum for other, less known, or even unpopular viewpoints. The opinion of an ordinary person who has had to make the decision to cut off life support from a terminally ill relative, for example, may be just as valuable and provide just as much insight as a medical ethicist's professional opinion. The editors have two additional purposes in including these less known views. One, the editors encourage readers to respect others' opinions—even when not enhanced by professional credibility. It is only by reading or listening to and objectively evaluating others' ideas that one can determine whether they are worthy of consideration. Two, the inclusion of such viewpoints encourages the important critical thinking skill of objectively evaluating an author's credentials and bias. This evaluation will illuminate an author's reasons for taking a particular stance on an issue and will aid in readers' evaluation of the author's ideas.

It is our hope that these books will give readers a deeper understanding of the issues debated and an appreciation of the complexity of even seemingly simple issues when good and honest people disagree. This awareness is particularly important in a democratic society such as ours in which people enter into public debate to determine the common good. Those with whom one disagrees should not be regarded as enemies but rather as people whose views deserve careful examination and may shed light on one's own.

Thomas Jefferson once said that "difference of opinion leads to inquiry, and inquiry to truth." Jefferson, a broadly educated man, argued that "if a nation expects to be ignorant and free . . . it expects what never was and never will be." As individuals and as a nation, it is imperative that we consider the opinions of others and examine them with skill and discernment. The Opposing Viewpoints Series is intended to help readers achieve this goal.

David L. Bender and Bruno Leone,
Founders

Greenhaven Press anthologies primarily consist of previously published material taken from a variety of sources, including periodicals, books, scholarly journals, newspapers, government documents, and position papers from private and public organizations. These original sources are often edited for length and to ensure their accessibility for a young adult audience. The anthology editors also change the original titles of these works in order to clearly present the main thesis of each viewpoint and to explicitly indicate the opinion presented in the viewpoint. These alterations are made in consideration of both the reading and comprehension levels of a young adult audience. Every effort is made to ensure that Greenhaven Press accurately reflects the original intent of the authors included in this anthology.

Introduction

"Regardless of their views on the moral or practical value of capital punishment, many Americans are now questioning the accuracy of convictions that lead to death sentences."

—*Facts On File News Service*

In 1982, nineteen-year-old Rebecca Williams was raped and murdered in her Virginia apartment. In the last minutes of her life, Williams was able to tell police that her attacker was a black man. Investigators eventually fingered Earl Washington Jr., an African American in his twenties who was arrested for an unrelated break-in and assault one year after the young woman's murder. When interrogated, Washington quickly confessed to the burglary, assault, rape, and homicide of Williams. Although he was found to have an IQ of 69—the mental level of a ten-year-old—Washington was convicted and sentenced to death in 1984.

Washington had served more than nine years on death row when early DNA tests cast doubt on his guilt—enough doubt to convince Virginia Governor Douglas Wilder to commute Washington's sentence to life in prison in 1994. By 2001, more definitive DNA tests revealed that some other convicted criminal had raped Williams, and Virginia's new Governor, James S. Gilmore, pardoned Washington, allowing his release from prison. Since this was the first time that freshly discovered evidence had freed a former death-row prisoner in that state, the case drew public curiosity and media attention. Many observers were shocked to learn that in 1985, Washington had come within days of execution before a prisoners' rights activist found him a lawyer to file his appeals. Perhaps more disturbing were the inconsistencies, investigative discrepancies, and attorney incompetence that many believe nearly led to the execution of an innocent man. Washington had been convicted largely on the basis of his 1983 confession, in which he stated that he had murdered a black woman who was alone. But Williams was white, and had been killed in the presence of two of her children. Washington had also claimed that he had stabbed the woman two or three times—but Williams had been stabbed thirty-eight times. Moreover, Washington had been unable to identify where Williams had lived. Columnist Richard Cohen explains that Washington "took the cops to one [apartment complex] then another until, finally, a kindly police officer pointed out where the murder had taken place. 'Oh yeah,' Washington must have said. He had a tendency to agree with police officers." In the murder trial that led to Washington's death sentence, the defense attorney had not informed the jury about any of these inconsistencies.

Earl Washington was not the first capital defendant to receive shoddy legal representation, a death sentence, and eventual exoneration through DNA evidence. Between 1976 and 2001, more than eighty death-row inmates nationwide were released from prison after charges against them were dropped due to wrongful convictions and overwhelming evidence of innocence. In January 2000, after more than half of the condemned inmates in Illinois had been declared innocent, pro–death penalty Governor George Ryan proclaimed a moratorium on all executions in that state. "I cannot support a system which, in its administration, has proven so fraught with error and has come so close to the ultimate nightmare, the state's taking of innocent life," Ryan stated.

In June 2000, a study conducted by a team of Columbia University lawyers found that two-thirds of all death sentences in the United States were based on "seriously flawed" convictions and were eventually overturned on appeal. This report—coupled with the Illinois moratorium—led many Americans to question whether the criminal justice system could be trusted to prevent the execution of innocents. According to a June 2000 Gallup Poll, 80 percent of Americans believe an innocent person has been executed since 1995; another survey found that 63 percent of Americans favor a suspension of executions until the fairness of capital trials can be determined. Consequently, some death penalty advocates have called for systemic reforms. The Illinois state Supreme Court, for example, has issued new rules to ensure that capital defendants receive adequate legal counsel. These measures assign at least two lawyers to poor defendants, require lead attorneys to have extensive felony trial experience, and ensure special training for judges who preside over capital cases. Critics, however, maintain that the abolition of the death penalty is the only way to keep innocents from being executed.

Some capital punishment supporters contend that the concerns about executing the innocent are unfounded. Commentator James Q. Wilson maintains that the Columbia University study actually proves that "a lot of death-penalty cases are reviewed over a long period of time—a fact that dramatically reduces the chances of innocent people having been executed. . . . We ought to calm down. No one has shown that innocent people are being executed." Others maintain that the furor over possible wrongful applications of the death penalty is being manipulated by activists who want to abolish capital punishment. In response to this, Detroit lawyer Stephen Markman argues that the possibility of executing the innocent does not justify the eradication of the death penalty: "The death penalty serves to protect a vastly greater number of innocent lives than are likely to be lost through its erroneous application. . . . A society would be guilty of a suicidal failure of nerve if it were to forego the use of an appropriate punishment simply because it is not humanly possible to eliminate the risk of mistake entirely." Wilson agrees, adding that critics of capital punishment "should make their views on the morality of execution clear and not rely on arguments about appeals . . . and the tiny chance that someday somebody innocent will be killed."

The issues raised in the case of Earl Washington Jr.—whether death sentences are handed out fairly and whether the criminal justice system should introduce significant reforms to prevent wrongful executions—have been debated for centuries. The first chapter of *The Death Penalty: Opposing Viewpoints* examines historical writings on the subject. The following chapters explore contemporary views on these questions: Is the Death Penalty Just? Is the Death Penalty an Effective Deterrent? Is the Death Penalty Applied Fairly? In this anthology, authors examine and debate the persisting controversies surrounding capital punishment.

Chapter 1

Three Centuries of Debate on the Death Penalty

Chapter Preface

Controversy over the death penalty is recent in the history of humankind. Most ancient societies accepted the idea that certain crimes deserved capital punishment. Ancient Roman and Mosaic law endorsed the notion of retaliation; they believed in the rule of "an eye for an eye." Similarly, the ancient Egyptians, Assyrians, and Greeks all executed citizens for a variety of offenses, ranging from perjury to murder.

Adherence to the death penalty continued into the Middle Ages, during which religious crimes such as sacrilege, heresy, and atheism were punishable by death. European settlers brought the death penalty to the American colonies, where idolatry, witchcraft, blasphemy, murder, sodomy, adultery, rape, perjury, and rebellion were all capital crimes in 1636. This continuing use of the death penalty reflected society's belief that severe crimes warranted severe punishments and that such punishments would deter others from committing such crimes.

This view was challenged during the Enlightenment of the eighteenth century, which dramatically altered European and American perceptions about social issues such as capital punishment. A movement to abolish or at least restrict the death penalty began to take shape in the writings of Cesare Beccaria, Montesquieu, Voltaire, and others. Their views were reflected in the words of American revolutionary Benjamin Rush in 1792: "The punishment of murder by death is contrary to reason, and to the order and happiness of society."

Other philosophers of this period, however, defended the death penalty. German philosopher Immanuel Kant asserted that the death penalty was the most equitable punishment for murder. Unremorseful murderers deserve to die, he believed, while remorseful, guilt-ridden murderers would welcome death as a relief from their emotional pain. The United States and most European nations continued to execute criminals, believing in its justness and in its deterrent effect.

Eighteenth-century philosophers such as Kant and Beccaria sparked a controversy that continued into the current century. The following chapter presents a variety of historical arguments supporting and opposing the death penalty.

VIEWPOINT 1

"Those who shew no mercy should find none; and if Hanging will not restrain them, Hanging them in Chains, and Starving them, or . . . breaking them on the Wheel . . . should."

The Death Penalty Will Discourage Crime (1701)

Paper Presented Before the English Parliament

In eighteenth-century England, some two hundred crimes were punishable by death, including pickpocketing and petty theft. Many people were attempting to reform this excess of executions by reducing the sentences for many offenses. Some believed, however, that the death penalty should continue to be rigorously applied for heinous crimes. In the following viewpoint, the author states that punishments should remain severe and perhaps be even more so. He argues that keeping the death penalty a very real threat is the only way to stop people from committing violent and offensive crimes.

As you read, consider the following questions:

1. Why does the author believe the death penalty must be used "steadily and impartially"?
2. On what does the author base his argument that there should be differences in the degrees of punishments?
3. What does the author say society should be careful of when applying the death penalty?

Hanging Not Punishment Enough for Murtherers, Highway Men, and House-Breakers. London: A. Balwin, 1701.

I am sensible, That the *English* Clemency and Mildness appear eminently in our Laws and Constitutions; but since it is found that *Ill* Men are grown so much more incorrigible, than in our fore-fathers Days, is it not fit that *Good* Men should grow less merciful to them, since gentler Methods are ineffectual?

I acknowledge also, That the Spirit of Christianity disposes us to Patience and Forbearance, insomuch that when the *Roman* Emperors began to grow Christian, we are informed, That most Capital Punishments were taken away, and turned into others less Sanguinary; either that they might have longer time for Repentance, (an Indulgence agreeable to the Zeal and Piety of those Good Ages) or that the length and continuance of their Punishment might be more Exemplary. And I acknowledge with the Wise *Quintilian, That if Ill men could be made Good, as, it must be granted, they sometimes may, it is for the Interest of the Commonwealth, that they should rather be spared than punished.* And I know, that 'tis frequently alledg'd, That you take away a Better thing, and that is a Man's Life, for that which is worse, and that is, your Money and Goods; but tho' this be speciously enough urged, yet I doubt not, but the Publick Safety and Happiness may lawfully and reasonably be secured by this way, if it can by no other. . . .

Show No Mercy to the Merciless

I must beg leave to say, that those who shew no mercy should find none; and if Hanging will not restrain them, Hanging them in Chains, and Starving them, or (if Murtherers and Robbers at the same time, or Night incendiaries) breaking them on the Wheel, or Whipping them to Death, a *Roman* Punishment should.

I know that Torments so unusual and unknown to us may at first surprize us, and appear unreasonable; but I hope easily to get over that difficulty, and make it appear upon Examination, that *that* will be the more probable way to secure us from our fears of them, and the means of preserving great numbers of them, who now yearly by an easie Death are taken off at the Gallows. For to Men so far corrupted in their Principles and Practices, and that have no expectations beyond the Grave (for such, I fear, is the case of most of them) no Argument will be so cogent, as Pain in an intense degree; and a few such Examples made, will be so terrifying, that I persuade myself it would be a Law but seldom put in Execution.

The Death Penalty Must Be Used

But then I must add, that I fear it will not have its due effects, if it be too often dispens'd with; since *that* will be apt to give ground to every Offender, to hope he may be of the number of *those*, who shall escape, and so the good end of the Law will be defeated. For if Favour or Affection, or a Man's being of a good Family, or Money can prevail, and take off the Penalty of the Statute; if it be not executed steadily and impartially, with an exact hand (still giving allowance for extraordinary Cases) it will serve to little purpose, since many will be found (as ill men easily flatter themselves) who will not fear a Law, that has sharp Teeth indeed, but does but sometimes bite. And this, I believe, must be allowed to be the only way to root out our Native Enemies, as they truly are; as might lately have been seen in a Neighbouring Kingdom, where severity, without the least mixture of mercy, did so sweep High-way Men out of the Nation, that it has been confidently said, that a Man might some time since have *openly* carried his Money without fear of losing it. That he cannot *now*, is to be charged upon their great numbers of Soldiers, without Employment and Plunder, and in poor pitiful Pay; and, it may be, on the very great necessities of the People, and make 'em desperate and careless of their Lives.

'Tis a Rule in Civil Law, and Reason, *That the Punishment should not exceed the fault*. If Death then be due to a Man, who surreptitiously steals the Value of Five Shillings (as it is made by a late Statute) surely *He* who puts me in fear of my Life, and breaks the King's Peace, and it may be, murthers me at last, and burns my House, deserves another sort of Censure; and if the one must die, the other should be made to *feel himself die*. . . .

The frequent Repetitions of the same Crimes, even in defiance of the present Laws in being, is a just ground of enacting somewhat more terrible; and indeed seems to challenge and require it.

Farther still; at the *last great day* doubtless there will be degrees of Torment, proportionable to Mens guilt and sin here; and I can see no reason why we may not imitate the Divine justice, and inflict an Animadversion suitable to such enormous Offenders.

Severe Penalties Prevent Crime

In England, Germany, and France, a man knows, that if he commit murder, every person around him will, from that instant, become his enemy, and use every means to seize him and bring him to justice. He knows that he will be immediately carried to prison, and put to an ignominious death, amidst the execrations of his countrymen. Impressed with these sentiments, and with the natural horror for murder which such sentiments augment, the populace of those countries hardly ever have recourse to stabbing in their accidental quarrels, however they may be inflamed with anger and rage. The lowest black-guard in the streets of London will not draw a knife against an antagonist far superior to himself in strength. He will fight him fairly with his fists as long as he can, and bear the severest drubbing, rather than use a means of defence which is held in detestation by his countrymen, and which would bring him to the gallows.

John Moore, *The Opinions of Different Authors upon the Punishment of Death*, 1812.

And this, I am persuaded, will best answer the End of Sanguinary Laws, which are not *chiefly* intended to punish the present Criminal, but to hinder others from being so; and on that account Punishments in the Learned Languages are called *Examples*, as being design'd to be such to all mankind. . . .

Careful of Shedding Human Blood

Still I am sensible, that tho' I argue for severity, in general ought to be tender of shedding human blood; For *there is such a Consanguinity and Relation between all mankind that no one ought to hurt another; unless for some good end to be obtain'd.* And *Bodily Punishment*, as the Civilian well observes, *is greater than any Pecuniary mulcts*; and every Man knows that he who loses his Life, is a much greater sufferer than he whose Goods are confiscated, or is Fined in the most unreasonable manner in the World.

But my design is not, that Man's blood *should* be shed, but that it should *not*; and I verily believe, that for *Five* Men Condemned and Executed *now*, you would hardly have *one then*. For those Men out of Terror of such a Law, would ('tis to be hoped) either apply themselves to honest Labour and Industry; or else would remove to our *Plantations*, where they are wanted, and so many useful Hands would not be yearly lost.

But I must add, That *it is not fit, that men in Criminal Causes*, as the Civil Law well directs, *should be condemned, unless the Evidence be clearer than the mid-day Sun*; and no Man should expire in such horrid Agonies, for whose Innocence there is the least pretense.

VIEWPOINT 2

"The punishment of death has never prevented determined men from injuring society."

The Death Penalty Will Not Discourage Crime (1764)

Cesare Beccaria

An Italian criminologist, Cesare Beccaria lived and died in the 1700s. He influenced local economic reforms and stimulated penal reform throughout Europe. In 1764 he published *An Essay on Crimes and Punishments*, one of the first arguments against capital punishment and inhumane treatment of criminals. In the following viewpoint, Beccaria condemns capital punishment on several grounds, including that it is not a deterrent to crime and is irrevocable.

As you read, consider the following questions:

1. Why does Beccaria believe that the death penalty may be justified if a man is a threat to government?
2. What does an execution inspire in others, according to the author? What does he say about this reaction?
3. What does Beccaria say about life imprisonment?

Cesare Beccaria, *An Essay on Crimes and Punishments*, originally published in London by F. Newberry, 1775.

The useless profusion of punishments, which has never made men better, induces me to enquire, whether the punishment of *death* be really just or useful in a well governed state? What *right*, I ask, have men to cut the throats of their fellow-creatures? Certainly not that on which the sovereignty and laws are founded. The laws, as I have said before, are only the sum of the smallest portions of the private liberty of each individual, and represent the general will, which is the aggregate of that of each individual. Did any one ever give to others the right of taking away his life? Is it possible, that in the smallest portions of the liberty of each, sacrificed to the good of the public, can be contained the greatest of all good, life? If it were so, how shall it be reconciled to the maxim which tells us, that a man has no right to kill himself? Which he certainly must have, if he could give it away to another.

But the punishment of death is not authorized by any right; for I have demonstrated that no such right exists. It is therefore a war of a whole nation against a citizen, whose destruction they consider as necessary, or useful to the general good. But if I can further demonstrate, that it is neither necessary nor useful, I shall have gained the cause of humanity.

Only One Reason for the Death Penalty

The death of a citizen cannot be necessary, but in one case. When, though deprived of his liberty, he has such power and connections as may endanger the security of the nation; when his existence may produce a dangerous revolution in the established form of government. But even in this case, it can only be necessary when a nation is on the verge of recovering or losing its liberty; or in times of absolute anarchy, when the disorders themselves hold the place of laws. But in a reign of tranquillity; in a form of government approved by the united wishes of the nation; in a state well fortified from enemies without, and supported by strength within, and opinion, perhaps more efficacious; where all power is lodged in the hands of a true sovereign; where riches can purchase pleasures and not authority, there can be no necessity for taking away the life of a subject.

If the experience of all ages be not sufficient to prove, that the punishment of death has never prevented determined men from injuring society; if the example of the Romans; if twenty years reign of Elizabeth, empress of Russia, in which she gave the fathers of their country an example more illustrious than many conquests bought with blood; if, I say, all this be not sufficient to persuade mankind, who always suspect the voice of reason, and who choose rather to be led by authority, let us consult human nature in proof of my assertion.

It is not the intenseness of the pain that has the greatest effect on the mind, but its continuance; for our sensibility is more easily and more powerfully affected by weak but repeated impressions, than by a violent, but momentary, impulse. The power of habits is universal over every sensible being. As it is by that we learn to speak, to walk, and to satisfy our necessities, so the ideas of morality are stamped on our minds by repeated impressions. The death of a criminal is a terrible but momentary spectacle, and therefore a less efficacious method of deterring others, than the continued example of a man deprived of his liberty, condemned, as a beast of burthen, to repair, by his labour, the injury he has done to society. *If I commit such a crime*, says the spectator to himself, *I shall be reduced to that miserable condition for the rest of my life.* A much more powerful preventive than the fear of death, which men always behold in distant obscurity.

A Dead Man Is Good for Nothing

It hath long since been observed, that a man after he is hanged is good for nothing, and that punishment invented for the good of society, ought to be useful to society. It is evident, that a score of stout robbers, condemned for life to some public work, would serve the state in their punishment, and that hanging them is a benefit to nobody but the executioner.

Commentary on Cesare Beccaria, attributed to Voltaire, c. 1770.

The terrors of death make so slight an impression, that it has not force enough to withstand the forgetfulness natural to mankind, even in the most essential things; especially when assisted by the passions. Violent impressions surprise us, but their effect is momentary; they are fit to produce those revolutions which instantly transform a common man into a Lacedaemonian or a Persian; but in a free and quiet government they ought to be rather frequent than strong.

The execution of a criminal is, to the multitude, a spectacle, which in some excites compassion mixed with indignation. These sentiments occupy the mind much more than that salutary terror which the laws endeavour to inspire; but in the contemplation of continued suffering, terror is the only, or [at] least predominant sensation. The severity of a punishment should be just sufficient to excite compassion in the spectators, as it is intended more for them than for the criminal.

A punishment, to be just, should have only that degree of severity which is sufficient to deter others. Now there is no man, who upon the least reflection, would put in competition total and perpetual loss of his liberty, with the greatest advantages he could possibly obtain in consequence of a crime. Perpetual slavery, then, has in it all that is necessary to deter the most hardened and determined, as much as the punishment of death. I say it has more. There are many who can look upon death with intrepidity and firmness; some through fanaticism, and others through vanity, which attends us even to the grave; others from a desperate resolution, either to get rid of their misery, or cease to live: but fanaticism and vanity forsake the criminal in slavery, in chains and fetters, in an iron cage; and despair seems rather the beginning than the end of their misery. The mind, by collecting itself and uniting all its force, can, for a moment, repel assailing grief; but its most vigorous efforts are insufficient to resist perpetual wretchedness.

In all nations, where death is used as a punishment, every example supposes a new crime committed. Whereas in perpetual slavery, every criminal affords a frequent and lasting example; and if it be necessary that men should often be witnesses of the power of the laws, criminals should often be put to death; but this supposes a frequency of crimes; and from hence this punishment will cease to have its effect, so that it must be useful and useless at the same time.

Slavery and the Death Penalty

I shall be told, that perpetual slavery is as painful a punishment as death, and therefore as cruel. I answer, that if all the miserable moments in the life of a slave were collected into one point, it would be a more cruel punishment than any other; but these are scattered through his whole life, whilst the pain of death exerts all its force in a moment. There is also another advantage in the punishment of slavery, which is, that it is more terrible to the spectator than to the sufferer himself; for the spectator considers the sum of all his wretched moments, whilst the sufferer, by the misery of the present, is prevented from thinking of the future. All evils are increased by the imagination, and the sufferer finds resources and consolations, of which the spectators are ignorant; who judge by their own sensibility of what passes in a mind, by habit grown callous to misfortune.

Let us, for a moment, attend to the reasoning of a robber or assassin, who is deterred from violating the laws by the gibbet or the wheel. I am sensible, that to develop the sentiments of one's own heart, is an art which education only can teach: but although a villain may not be able to give a clear account of his principles, they nevertheless influence his conduct. He reasons thus:

> What are these laws, that I am bound to respect, which make so great a difference between me and the rich man? He refuses me the farthing I ask of him, and excuses himself, by bidding me have recourse to labour with which he is unacquainted. Who made these laws? The rich and the great, who never deigned to visit the miserable hut of the poor; who have never seen him dividing a piece of mouldly bread, amidst the cries of his famished children and the tears of his wife. Let us break those ties, fatal to the greatest part of mankind, and only useful to a few indolent tyrants. Let us attack injustice at its source. I will return to my natural state of independence. I shall live free and happy on the fruits of my courage and industry. A day of pain and repentance may come, but it will be short; and for an hour of grief I shall enjoy years of pleasure and liberty. King of a small number, as determined as myself, I will correct the mistakes of fortune; and I shall see those tyrants grow pale and tremble at the sight of him, whom, with insulting pride, they would not suffer to rank with their dogs and horses.

Religion then presents itself to the mind of this lawless villain, and promising him almost a certainty of eternal happiness upon the easy terms of repentance, contributes much to lessen the horror of the last scene of the tragedy.

Horrible Punishments Serve No Purpose

A government that persists in retaining these horrible punishments can only assign one reason in justification of their conduct: that they have already so degraded and brutalized the habits of the people, that they cannot be restrained by any moderate punishments.

Are more atrocities committed in those countries where such punishments are unknown? Certainly not: the most savage banditti are always to be found under laws the most severe, and it is no more than what might be expected. The fate with which they are threatened hardens them to the sufferings of others as well as to their own. They know that they can expect no lenity, and they consider their acts of cruelty as retaliations.

Jeremy Bentham, *The Opinions of Different Authors on the Punishment of Death*, 1809.

But he who foresees, that he must pass a great number of years, even his whole life, in pain and slavery; a slave to those laws by which he was protected; in sight of his fellow citizens, with whom he lives in freedom and society; makes an useful comparison between those evils, the uncertainty of his success, and the shortness of the time in which he shall enjoy the fruits of his transgression. The example of those wretches continually before his eyes, make a much greater impression on him than a punishment, which, instead of correcting, makes him more obdurate.

The punishment of death is pernicious to society, from the example of barbarity it affords. If the passions, or the necessity of war, have taught men to shed the blood of their fellow creatures, the laws, which are intended to moderate the ferocity of mankind, should not increase it by examples of barbarity, the more horrible, as this punishment is usually attended with formal pageantry. Is it not absurd, that the laws, which detest and punish homicide, should, in order to prevent murder, publicly commit murder themselves? . . .

Seeking Truth

If it be objected, that almost all the nations in all ages have punished certain crimes with death, I answer, that the force of these examples vanishes, when opposed to truth, against which prescription is urged in vain. The history of mankind is an immense sea of errors, in which a few obscure truths may here and there be found.

But human sacrifices have also been common in almost all nations. That some societies only, either few in number, or for a very short time, abstained from the punishment of death, is rather favourable to my argument, for such is the fate of great truths, that their duration is only as a flash of lightning in the long and dark night of error. The happy time is not yet arrived, when truth, as falsehood has been hitherto, shall be the portion of the greatest number.

"We show . . . our regard for [human life] by the adoption of a rule that he who violates that right in another forfeits it for himself."

Society Must Retain the Death Penalty for Murder (1868)

John Stuart Mill

John Stuart Mill, prominent philosopher and economist, is probably best known as the author of the famous essay *On Liberty*. From 1865 to 1868 he served as a member of the British Parliament and constantly advocated political and social reforms such as emancipation for women, and the development of labor organizations and farm cooperatives. In the following viewpoint, taken from a Parliamentary Debate on April 21, 1868, Mill argues that while he is an advocate for lesser penalties for crimes such as theft, society must retain the death penalty for crimes of murder.

As you read, consider the following questions:

1. Why does the author argue that the death penalty is the most humane alternative for the criminal?
2. Does the death penalty deter crime, according to Mill?
3. Why does the author say he disagrees with the philanthropists on the issue of the death penalty?

John Stuart Mill, *Hansard's Parliamentary Debate*, 3rd Series, London: April 21, 1868.

It is always a matter of regret to me to find myself, on a public question, opposed to those who are called—sometimes in the way of honour, and sometimes in what is intended for ridicule— the philanthropists. Of all persons who take part in public affairs, they are those for whom, on the whole, I feel the greatest amount of respect; for their characteristic is, that they devote their time, their labour, and much of their money to objects purely public, with a less admixture of either personal or class selfishness, than any other class of politicians whatever. On almost all the great questions, scarcely any politicians are so steadily and almost uniformly to be found on the side of right; and they seldom err, but by an exaggerated application of some just and highly important principle. On the very subject that is now occupying us we all know what signal service they have rendered. It is through their efforts that our criminal laws . . . have so greatly relaxed their most revolting and most impolitic ferocity, that aggravated murder is now practically the only crime which is punished with death by any of our lawful tribunals; and we are even now deliberating whether the extreme penalty should be retained in that solitary case. This vast gain, not only to humanity, but to the ends of penal justice, we owe to the philanthropists; and if they are mistaken, as I cannot but think they are, in the present instance, it is only in not perceiving the right time and place for stopping in a career hitherto so eminently beneficial. Sir, there is a point at which, I conceive, that career ought to stop.

Just Penalty for Some Circumstances

When there has been brought home to any one, by conclusive evidence, the greatest crime known to the law; and when the attendant circumstances suggest no palliation of the guilt, no hope that the culprit may even yet not be unworthy to live among mankind, nothing to make it probable that the crime was an exception to his general character rather than a consequence of it, then I confess it appears to me that to deprive the criminal of the life of which he has proved himself to be unworthy— solemnly to blot him out from the fellowship of mankind and from the catalogue of the living—is the most appropriate, as it is certainly the most impressive, mode in which society can attach to so great a crime the penal consequences which for the security of life it is indispensable to annex to it. I defend this penalty, when confined to atrocious cases, on the very ground on which it is commonly attacked—on that of humanity to the criminal; as beyond comparison the least cruel mode in which it is possible adequately to deter from the crime. If, in our horror of inflicting death, we endeavour to devise some punishment for the living criminal which shall act on the human mind with a deterrent force at all comparable to that of death, we are driven to inflictions less severe indeed in appearance, and therefore less efficacious, but far more cruel in reality.

The Most Powerful Deterrent

The punishment of death is unquestionably the most powerful deterrent, the most effective preventive, that can be applied. Human nature teaches this fact. An instinct that outruns all reasoning, a dreadful horror that overcomes all other sentiments, works in us all when we contemplate it.

Samuel Hand, *The North American Review*, December 1881.

Few, I think, would venture to propose, as a punishment for aggravated murder, less than imprisonment with hard labour for life; that is the fate to which a murderer would be consigned by the mercy which shrinks from putting him to death. But has it been sufficiently considered what sort of a mercy this is, and what kind of life it leaves to him? If, indeed, the punishment is not really inflicted—if it becomes the sham which a few years ago such punishments were rapidly becoming—then, indeed, its adoption would be almost tantamount to giving up the attempt to repress murder altogether. But if it really is what it professes to be, and if it is realized in all its rigour by the popular imagination, as it very probably would not be, but as it must be if it is to be efficacious, it will be so shocking that when the memory of the crime is no longer fresh, there will be almost insuperable difficulty in executing it. What comparison can there really be, in point of severity, between consigning a man to the short pang of a rapid death, and immuring him in a living tomb, there to linger out what may be a long life in the hardest and most monotonous toil, without any of its alleviations or rewards—debarred from all pleasant sights and sounds, and cut off from all earthly hope, except a slight mitigation of bodily restraint, or a small improvement of diet? Yet even such a lot as this, because there is no one moment at which the suffering is of terrifying intensity, and, above all, because it does not contain the element, so imposing to the imagination, of the unknown, is universally reputed a milder punishment than death—stands in all codes as a mitigation of the capital penalty, and is thankfully accepted as such. For it is characteristic of all punishments which depend on duration for their efficacy—all, therefore, which are not corporal or pecuniary—that they are more rigorous than they seem; while it is, on the contrary, one of the strongest recommendations a punishment can have, that it should seem more rigorous than it is; for its practical power depends far less on what it is than on what it seems.

There is not, I should think, any human infliction which makes an impression on the imagination so entirely out of proportion to its real severity as the punishment of death. The punishment must be mild indeed which does not add more to the sum of human misery than is necessarily or directly added by the execution of a criminal. . . . The most that human laws can do to anyone in the matter of death is to hasten it; the man would have died at any rate; not so very much later, and on the average, I fear, with a considerably greater amount of bodily suffering. Society is asked, then, to denude itself of an instrument of punishment which, in the grave cases to which alone it is suitable, effects its purpose at a less cost of human suffering than any other; which, while it inspires more terror, is less cruel in actual fact than any punishment that we should think of substituting for it. My hon. Friend [Mr. Gilpin] says that it does not inspire terror, and that experience proves it to be a failure. But the influence of a punishment is not to be estimated by its effect on hardened criminals. Those whose habitual way of life keeps them, so to speak, at all times within sight of the gallows, do grow to care less about it; as, to compare good things with bad, an old soldier is not much affected by the chance of dying in battle. I can afford to admit all that is often said about the indifference of professional criminals to the gallows.

Though of that indifference one-third is probably bravado and another third confidence that they shall have the luck to escape, it is quite probable that the remaining third is real. But the efficacy of a punishment which acts principally through the imagination, is chiefly to be measured by the impression it makes on those who are still innocent: by the horror with which it surrounds the first promptings of guilt; the restraining influence it exercises over the beginning of the thought which, if indulged, would become a temptation; the check which it exerts over the gradual declension towards the state—never suddenly attained—in which crime no longer revolts, and punishment no longer terrifies.

Unknown Number of Lives Saved

As for what is called the failure of death punishment, who is able to judge of that? We partly know who those are whom it has not deterred; but who is there who knows whom it has deterred, or how many human beings it has saved who would have lived to be murderers if that awful association had not been thrown round the idea of murder from their earliest infancy? Let us not forget that the most imposing fact loses its power over the imagination if it is made too cheap. When a punishment fit only for the most atrocious crimes is lavished on small offences until human feeling recoils from it, then, indeed, it ceases to intimidate, because it ceases to be believed in.

Deserved Retribution

Capital execution upon the deadly poisoner and the midnight assassin is not only necessary for the safety of society, it is the fit and deserved retribution of their crimes. By it alone is divine and human justice fulfilled.

Samuel Hand, *The North American Review*, December 1881.

The failure of capital punishment in cases of theft is easily accounted for: the thief did not believe that it would be inflicted. He had learnt by experience that jurors would perjure themselves rather than find him guilty; that Judges would seize any excuse for not sentencing him to death, or for recommending him to mercy; and that if neither jurors nor Judges were merciful, there were still hopes from an authority above both. When things had come to this pass it was high time to give up the vain attempt. When it is impossible to inflict a punishment, or when its infliction becomes a public scandal, the idle threat cannot too soon disappear from the statute book. And in the case of the host of offences which were formerly capital, I heartily rejoice that it did become impracticable to execute the law.

If the same state of public feeling comes to exist in the case of murder; if the time comes when jurors refuse to find a murderer guilty; when Judges will not sentence him to death, or will recommend him to mercy; or when, if juries and Judges do not flinch from their duty, Home Secretaries, under pressure of deputations and memorials, shrink from theirs, and the threat becomes, as it became in the other cases, a mere *brutum fulmen;* then, indeed, it may become necessary to do in this case what has been done in those—to abrogate the penalty. That time may come—my hon. Friend thinks that it has nearly come. I hardly know whether he lamented it or boasted of it; but he and his Friends are entitled to the boast: for if it comes it will be their doing, and they will have gained what I cannot but call a fatal victory, for they will have achieved it by bringing about, if they will forgive me for saying so, an enervation, an effeminacy, in the general mind of the country. For what else than effeminacy is it to be so much more shocked by taking a man's life than by depriving him of all that makes life desirable or valuable? Is death, then, the greatest of all earthly ills? *Usque adeone mori miserum est?* [Is it, indeed, so dreadful a thing to die?] Has it not been from of old one chief part of a manly education to make us despise death—teaching us to account it, if an evil at all, by no means high in the list of evils; at all events, as an inevitable one, and to hold, as it were, our lives in our hands, ready to be given or risked at any moment, for a sufficiently worthy object? I am sure that my hon. Friends know all this as well, and have as much of all these feelings as any of the rest of us; possibly more. But I cannot think that this is likely to be the effect of their teaching on the general mind.

The Value of Human Life

I cannot think that the cultivating of a peculiar sensitiveness of conscience on this one point, over and above what result from the general cultivation of the moral sentiments, is permanently consistent with assigning in our own minds to the fact of death no more than the degree of relative importance which belongs to it among the other incidents of our humanity. The men of old cared too little about death, and gave their own lives or took those of others with equal recklessness. Our danger is of the opposite kind, lest we should be so much shocked by death, in general and in the abstract, as to care too much about it in individual cases, both those of other people and our own, which call for its being risked. And I am not putting things at the worst, for it is proved by the experience of other countries that horror of the executioner by no means necessarily implies horror of the assassin. The stronghold, as we all know, of hired assassination in the 18th century was Italy; yet it is said that in some of the Italian populations the infliction of death by sentence of law was in the highest degree offensive and revolting to popular feeling. Much has been said of the sanctity of human life, and the absurdity of supposing that we can teach respect for life by ourselves destroying it. But I am surprised at the employment of this argument, for it is one which might be brought against any punishment whatever. It is not human life only, not human life as such, that ought to be sacred to us, but human feelings. The human capacity of suffering is what we should cause to be respected, not the mere capacity of existing. And we may imagine somebody asking how we can teach people not to inflict suffering by ourselves inflicting it? But to this I should answer—all of us would answer—that to deter by suffering from inflicting suffering is not only possible, but the very purpose of penal justice. Does fining a criminal show want of respect for property, or imprisoning him, for personal freedom? Just as unreasonable is it to think that to take the life of a man who has taken that of another is to show want of regard for human life. We show, on the contrary, most emphatically our regard for it, by the adoption of a rule that he who violates that right in another forfeits it for himself, and that while no other crime that he can commit deprives him of his right to live, this shall.

There is one argument against capital punishment, even in extreme cases, which I cannot deny to have weight. . . . It is this—that if by an error of justice an innocent person is put to death, the mistake can never be corrected; all compensation, all reparation for the wrong is impossible. This would be indeed a serious objection if these miserable mistakes—among the most tragical occurrences in the whole round of human affairs—could not be made extremely rare. The argument is invincible where the mode of criminal procedure is dangerous to the innocent, or where the Courts of Justice are not trusted. And this probably is the reason why the objection to an irreparable punishment began (as I believe it did) earlier, and is more intense and more widely diffused, in some parts of the Continent of Europe than it is here. There are on the continent great and enlightened countries, in which the criminal procedure is not so favourable to innocence, does not afford the same security against erroneous conviction, as it does among us; countries where the Courts of Justice seem to think they fail in their duty unless they find somebody guilty; and in their really laudable desire to hunt guilt from its hiding-places, expose themselves to a serious danger of condemning the innocent. If our own procedure and Courts of Justice afforded ground for similar apprehension, I should be the first to join in withdrawing the power of inflicting irreparable punishment from such tribunals. But we all know that the defects of our procedure are the very opposite.

Perish the Murderers

It is better that the murderer should perish than that innocent men and women should have their throats cut. A witty Frenchman lately wrote a pamphlet on this subject, and said—

> "I am all for abolishing the penalty of death, if Messieurs the Assassins would only set the example."

Mr. Gregory, from debate before England's Parliament, April 21, 1868.

Our rules of evidence are even too favourable to the prisoner: and juries and Judges carry out the maxim, "It is better that ten guilty should escape than that one innocent person should suffer," not only to the letter, but beyond the letter. Judges are most anxious to point out, and juries to allow for, the barest possibility of the prisoner's innocence. No human judgment is infallible: such sad cases as my hon. Friend cited will sometimes occur; but in so grave a case as that of murder, the accused, in our system, has always the benefit of the merest shadow of a doubt. And this suggests another consideration very germane to the question. The very fact that death punishment is more shocking than any other to the imagination, necessarily renders the courts of Justice more scrupulous in requiring the fullest evidence of guilt. Even that which is the greatest objection to capital punishment, the impossibility of correcting an error once committed, must make, and does make, juries and Judges more careful in forming their opinion, and more jealous in their scrutiny of the evidence.

If the substitution of penal servitude for death in cases of murder should cause any relaxation in this conscientious scrupulosity, there would be a great evil to set against the real, but I hope rare, advantage of being able to make reparation to a condemned person who was afterwards discovered to be innocent. In order that the possibility of correction may be kept open wherever the chance of this sad contingency is more than infinitesimal, it is quite right that the Judge should recommend to the Crown a commutation of the sentence, not solely when the proof of guilt is open to the smallest suspicion, but whenever there remains anything unexplained and mysterious in the case, raising a desire for more light, or making it likely that further information may at some future time be obtained.

Against Total Abolition

I would also suggest that whenever the sentence is commuted the grounds of the commutation should, in some authentic form, be made known to the public. Thus much I willingly concede to my hon. Friend; but on the question of total abolition I am inclined to hope that the feeling of the country is not with him, and that the limitation of death punishment to the cases referred to in the Bill of last year will be generally considered sufficient. The mania which existed a short time ago for paring down all our punishments seems to have reached its limits, and not before it was time. We were in danger of being left without any effectual punishment, except for small offences. . . .

I think . . . that in the case of most offences, except those against property, there is more need of strengthening our punishments than of weakening them: and that severer sentences, with an apportionment of them to the different kinds of offences which shall approve itself better than at present to the moral sentiments of the community, are the kind of reform of which our penal system now stands in need.

Viewpoint

"Putting men to death in cold blood by human law . . . seems to me a most pernicious and brutalizing practice."

The Death Penalty Is State-Sanctioned Murder (1872)

Horace Greeley

Horace Greeley is a true American success story. Having grown up in abject poverty and with little education, Greeley founded the *New York Tribune* in 1841 and made it one of the most influential papers in the country. A social reformer, Greeley advocated temperance, women's rights, and a homestead law. In the following viewpoint Greeley addresses four points he believes prove the death penalty is dangerous and brutal.

As you read, consider the following questions:

1. Why does the author argue the death penalty is obsolete?
2. Why does Greeley believe the death penalty sanctions revenge?

Horace Greeley, *Hints Toward Reforms in Lectures, Addresses, and Other Writings.* New York: Harper & Brothers, 1850.

Is it ever justifiable . . . to [kill] malefactors by sentence of law? I answer Yes, *provided* Society can in no other way be secured against a repetition of the culprit's offence. In committing a murder, for instance, he has proved himself capable of committing more murders—perhaps many. The possibility of a thousand murders is developed in his one act of felonious homicide. Call his moral state depravity, insanity, or whatever you please, he is manifestly a ferocious, dangerous animal, who can not safely be permitted to go at large. Society must be secured against the reasonable probability of his killing others, and, where that can only be effected by taking his life, his life must be taken.

—But suppose him to be in New-England, New-York or Pennsylvania—arrested, secured and convicted—Society's rebel, outcast and prisoner of war—taken with arms in his hands. Here are prison-cells wherefrom escape is impossible; and if there be any fear of his assaulting his keeper or others, that may be most effectively prevented. Is it expedient or salutary to crush the life out of this helpless, abject, pitiable wretch?

A Sorrowful Mistake

I for one think it decidedly *is not*—that it is a sorrowful mistake and barbarity to do any such thing. In saying this, I do not assume to decide whether Hanging or Imprisonment for Life is the severer penalty. I should wish to understand clearly the moral state of the prisoner before I attempted to guess; and, even then, I know too little of the scenes of untried being which lie next beyond the confines of this mortal existence to say whether it were better for any penitent or hardened culprit to be hung next month or left in prison to die a natural death. What is best for that culprit I leave to God, who knows when is the fit time for him to die. My concern is with Society—the moral it teaches, the conduct it tacitly enjoins. And I feel that the choking to death of this culprit works harm, in these respects, namely:

1. *It teaches and sanctions Revenge.* There is a natural inclination in man to return injury for injury, evil for evil. It is the exciting cause of many murders as well as less flagrant crimes. It stands in no need of stimulation—its prompt re-

pression at all times is one of the chief trials even of good men. But A.B. has committed a murder, is convicted of and finally hung for it. Bill, Dick and Jim, three apprentices of ordinary understanding and attainments, beg away or run away to witness the hanging. Ask either of them, 'What is this man hung for?' and the prompt, correct answer will be, 'Because he killed C.D.'—not 'To prevent his killing others,' nor yet 'To prevent others from killing.' Well: the three enjoy the spectacle and turn away satisfied. On their way home, a scuffle is commenced in fun, but gradually changes to a fight, wherein one finds himself down with two holding and beating him. Though sorely exasperated and severely suffering, he can not throw them off, but he can reach with one hand the knife in his vest pocket. Do you fancy he will be more or less likely to use it because of that moral spectacle which Society has just proffered for his delectation and improvement? You may say Less if you can, but I say More! many times more! You may preach to him that Revenge is right for Society but wrong for him till your head is gray, and he perhaps may listen to you—but not till after he has opened his knife and made a lunge with it.

Death Penalty Unnecessary

It is not necessary to hang the murderer in order to guard society against him, and to prevent him from repeating the crime. If it were, we should hang the maniac, who is the most dangerous murderer. Society may defend itself by other means than by destroying life. Massachusetts can build prisons strong enough to secure the community forever against convicted felons.

Robert Rantoul Jr., *Report to the Legislature,* 1836.

2. *It tends to weaken and destroy the natural horror of bloodshed.* Man has a natural horror of taking the life of his fellow man. His instincts revolt at it—his conscience condemns it—his frame shudders at the thought of it. But let him see first one and then another strung up between heaven and earth and choked to death, with due formalities of Law and solemnities of Religion— the slayer not accounted an evildoer but an executor of the State's just decree, a pillar of the

Social edifice—and his horror of bloodshed *per se* sensibly and rapidly oozes away, and he comes to look at killing men as quite the thing provided there be adequate reason for it. But what reason? and whose? The law slays the slayer; but in his sight the corrupter or calumniator of his wife or sister, the traducer of his character, the fraudulent bankrupt who has involved and ruined his friend, is every whit as great a villain as the man-slayer, and deserving of as severe a punishment. Yet the Law makes no provision for such punishment—hardly for any punishment at all—and what shall he do? He can not consent that the guilty go 'unwhipt of justice,' so he takes his rifle and deals out full measure of it. He is but doing as Society has taught him by example. War, dueling, bloody affrays, &c., find their nourishment and support in the Gallows.

3. *It facilitates and often insures the escape of the guilty from any punishment by human law.*—Jurors (whether for or against Capital Punishment) dread to convict where the crime is Death. Human judgment is fallible; human testimony may mislead. Witnesses often lie—sometimes conspire to lie plausibly and effectively. Circumstances often strongly point to a conclusion which is after all a false one. The real murderers sometimes conspire to fasten suspicion on some innocent person, and so arrange the circumstances that he can hardly escape their toils. Sometimes they appear in court as witnesses against him, and swear the crime directly upon him. A single legal work contains a list of one hundred cases in which men were hung for crimes which they were afterward proved entirely innocent of. And for every such case there have doubtless been many wherein juries, unwilling to take life where there was a *possibility* of innocence, have given the prisoner the benefit of a very faint doubt and acquitted him. Had the penalty been Imprisonment, they would have convicted, notwithstanding the bare possibility of his innocence, since any future developments in his favor, through the retraction of witnesses, the clearing up of circumstances, or the confession of the actual culprit, would at once lead to his liberation and to an earnest effort by the community to repay him for his unmerited ignominy and suffering. But choke the prisoner to death, and any development in his fa-

Capital Punishment

Paul Conrad, ©1985, *Los Angeles Times*. Reprinted with permission.

vor is thenceforth too late. Next year may prove him innocent beyond cavil nor doubt; but of what avail is that to the victim over whose grave the young grass is growing? And thus, through the inexorable character of the Death-Penalty, hundreds of the innocent suffer an undeserved and ignominious death, while tens of thousands of the guilty escape any punishment by human law.

Sympathizing with the Criminal

4. *It excites a pernicious sympathy for the convict.*—We ought ever to be merciful toward the sinful and guilty, remember-

ing our own misdeeds and imperfections. We ought to regard with a benignant compassion those whom Crime has doomed to suffer. But the criminal is not a hero, nor a martyr, and should not be made to resemble one. A crowd of ten to fifty thousand persons, witnessing the infliction of the law's just penalty on an offender, and half of them sobbing and crying from sympathy for his fate, is not a wholesome spectacle—far otherwise. The impression it makes is not that of the majesty and Divine benignity of Law—the sovereignty and beneficence of Justice. Thousands are hoping, praying, entreating that a pardon may yet come—some will accuse the Executive of cruelty and hardness of heart in withholding it. While this furnace of sighs is at red heat, this tempest of sobs in full career, the culprit is swung off—a few faint; many shudder; more feel an acute shock of pain; while the great mass adjourn to take a general drink, some of them swearing that *this* hanging was a great shame—that the man did not really deserve it. Do you fancy the greater number have imbibed and will profit by the intended lesson?

—But I do not care to pile argument on argument, consideration on consideration, in opposition to the expediency, in this day and section, of putting men to death in cold blood by human law. It seems to me a most pernicious and brutalizing practice. Indeed, the recent enactments of our own, with most if not all of the Free States, whereby Executions are henceforth to take place in private, or in the presence of a few select witnesses only, seem clearly to admit the fact. They certainly imply that Executions are of no use as examples—that they rather tend to make criminals than to reform those already depraved. When I see any business or vocation sneaking and skulking in dark lanes and little by-streets which elude observation, I conclude that those who follow such business feel at least doubtful of its utility and beneficence. They may *argue* that it is 'a necessary evil,' but they can hardly put faith in their own logic. When I see the bright array of many-colored liquor bottles, which formerly filled flauntingly the post of honor in every tip-top hotel, now hustled away into some sideroom, and finally down into a dark basement, out of the sight and knowledge of all but those who especially seek them, I say exultingly, 'Good for so much! one more 'hoist, and they will be—where they should be—out of sight 'and reach altogether:'—so, when I see the Gallows, once the denizen of some swelling eminence, the cynosure of ten thousand eyes, 'the observed of all observers,' skulking and hiding itself from public view in jail-yards, shutting itself up in prisons, I say, 'You have taken the right road! Go 'ahead! One more drive, and your detested, rickety frame 'is out of the sight of civilized man for ever!'

VIEWPOINT

"It is the finality of the death penalty which instils fear into the heart of every murderer, and it is this fear of punishment which protects society."

Capital Punishment Is a Safeguard for Society (1925)

Robert E. Crowe

In early 1925, when Judge Robert E. Crowe wrote his opinion of the death penalty, he was state's attorney for Cook County, Illinois. He had just been the prosecutor in the widely publicized trial of Nathan Leopold and Richard Loeb, two young men who were charged with the murder of a young boy. The first World War had not been over for long and America was beginning to focus again on its own growing problem of crime. In this viewpoint Crowe defends the American legal system and the necessity of ridding society of murderers in order to secure safety for its members and deter further murders.

As you read, consider the following questions:

1. Why does the author believe that a murderer is a danger to all of society?
2. How does Crowe think the American system protects the accused criminal?
3. What arguments does the author offer for his statement that capital punishment is a deterrent to crime?

Robert E. Crowe, "Capital Punishment Protects Society," *The Forum*, February 1925.

I believe that the penalty for murder should be death. I urge capital punishment for murder not because I believe that society wishes to take the life of a murderer but because society does not wish to lose its own. I advocate this extreme and irrevocable penalty because the punishment is commensurate with the crime. The records, I believe, will show that the certainty of punishment is a deterrent of crime. As the law is written in most of the States of the Union, every other form of punishment is revocable at the will of an individual.

It is the finality of the death penalty which instils fear into the heart of every murderer, and it is this fear of punishment which protects society. Murderers are not punished for revenge. The man with the life blood of another upon his hands is a menace to the life of every citizen. He should be removed from society for the sake of society. In his removal, society is sufficiently protected, but only provided it is a permanent removal. I should like to see the experiment of the inexorable infliction of the death penalty upon all deliberate murderers tried out in every State of the Union for a sufficient period of time to demonstrate whether or not it is the most effective and most certain means of checking the appalling slaughter of innocent, peaceful, and law-abiding citizens which has gone on without check for so many years, and which is increasing at a rate which has won for the United States of America the disgrace of being known as "the most lawless nation claiming place among the civilized nations of the world."

Duty to Society

The attitude which society must take toward offenders—great as well as small—must not be confused with the attitude which the individual quite properly may assume. Neither may officers of the law nor leaders of public thought, if they are mindful of the duty which they owe to society, advocate a substitution of any other penalty for murder than that penalty which will give to society the greatest degree of protection. . . .

In cases where—in a properly constituted court over whose deliberations a properly elected or appointed judge has presided and in which, after hours and days and sometimes weeks of patient and deliberate inquiry, a jury of twelve men selected in the manner which the law provides—a man charged with murder has been found guilty and sentenced to death, it is an unpardonable abuse of the great power of executive clemency to nullify the verdict by commuting the sentence to life imprisonment. It is in effect a usurpation by the executive authority of the state of powers and duties deliberately and expressly assigned by the representatives of the people in the constitution to the judicial branch alone.

I do not believe that the American Bar is ready to plead guilty to the charge which this action infers that lawyers for the prosecution and lawyers for the defense are so venal, corrupt, and bloodthirsty through ulterior motives as to deliberately conspire with an unrighteous judge, an unprincipled or irresponsible jury and witnesses prompted solely by the spirit of revenge to doom to death any man on a charge of murder unless the testimony truly shows him guilty beyond all reasonable doubt. . . .

Faith in Americans

It is because of my faith and trust in the integrity of our American citizens that I believe that there is no considerable danger that the innocent man will be convicted and that society may be charged that in a blind zeal to protect itself against murder it actually commits murder by the infliction of the death penalty.

The man who kills is society's greatest enemy. He has set up his own law. He is an anarchist—the foe of all civilized government. If anarchy is not to be met with anarchy, it must be met by the laws, and these laws must be enforced. . . .

Why are there so few violations of the laws of the United States? When a man files his income tax schedule, why does he hire an auditor to see that he makes no mistake, and why does the same man when he goes before our Boards of Assessors and Boards of Review and schedules his personal property for taxation in Chicago as well as elsewhere conceal millions upon which he should be taxed? Why? Because when you get into the United States court after having violated the laws of the United States, if you are guilty, no plea of mercy, however eloquent or by whomsoever delivered, will cheat the law there.

We hear much about England. There murder is murder. Justice is swift and sure. There are fewer murders in the entire Kingdom of Great Britain yearly than there are in the city of Chicago.

Penalize Offenders

If we want order, we must stop being soft-headed sentimentalists when it comes to penalizing offenders. The murder rate in the United States rises to a scandalous figure. Of the many who kill, comparatively few are ever arrested, still fewer convicted, fewer yet ever see the inside of a felon's cell; only rarely is the murderer punished as the law says he shall be. A life term is commonly a short vacation at State expense with nothing to do but eat the fruit of others' industry. Americans are not a nation of murder lovers. We merely seem to be. We are made to seem to be by ill-prepared judges, woozy jurors, and a public opinion sentimentally inclined to sympathize more with the perpetrators than the victims of major crimes. This country needs a rededication to the everlasting truth that the fear of prompt and adequate punishment is the best deterrent for gentlemen tempted to slay. This violates long book-shelves of theory.

Cleveland Plain Dealer, January 25, 1925.

In recent years the American public has been influenced to some extent by an active, persistent, and systematic agitation based upon an unfortunate and misplaced sympathy for persons accused of crime. I say unfortunate and misplaced sympathy because it is a sympathy guided by emotion and impulse rather than upon reason and compassion for the prisoners at the bar. It is so deep and soul stirring that it loses its sense of proportion. It forgets the life that was blotted out. It forgets the broken-hearted left behind. It forgets the fatherless and sometimes homeless children which should be the real object of pity. It forgets that they become charges upon the state and it also forgets that there has been established a broken home—the one in the group of homes from which twice as many criminals come as from those which remain intact.

Opponents of capital punishment think somewhat along the same lines. They forget that murder is inexorable and that the victim never returns. They forget that society is protected best by punishment which is proportionate to the crime. They are moved to abolish hanging because it is an unwholesome spectacle. They overlook the unwholesome and harrowing aspects of a murder scene.

Some who admit the justice of capital punishment deny its necessity. They argue that in taking the life of an offender society is wreaking vengeance upon a helpless individual, while, as a matter of fact, the exact opposite is true. If an individual were to slay another who was guilty of murder, especially if he had no fear of him, the act would be prompted by revenge. And when we realize that many of our present-day murderers are professional criminals whose victims were slain in the course of holdups, robberies, and other crimes committed for profit, and that the victim was killed deliberately on the theory that dead men can make no identifications, we know at once that they did not kill for revenge and that they had no malice against the individual they killed. Society for its own protection should make it impossible for these men to kill again.

Crime Against Society

Murder like all other crime is a crime against society. It is for assault upon society that the state inflicts punishment. Too many confuse the relation of the victim of a crime with that of the interest of the state in the prosecution of criminals. The state is impersonal. It is the voice for all of the people expressed by a voting majority. What happens or has happened to any individual is not of great importance. The civil courts exist for the adjudication of the individual and personal wrong. The criminal court exists to punish those who have offended against the state. He who violates the criminal code offends against and injures us all. When he injures to the extent of unlawfully taking human life, he has committed a grave and irreparable injury.

Punishment of the slayer will not bring back life to the victim. But punishment for crime is not inflicted upon any theory of relationship to the victim except to consider the fact that the victim was a part of society and that in wronging the individual that society itself has been assaulted.

Responsibility for Actions

I am not ready to agree to the theory that all or most murderers are not responsible for their acts. I believe that man is entitled to free will and that except in rare instances he is both morally and legally responsible for all his acts. I cannot accept the theory that murderers should not be punished for their crime because they are irresponsible. If they are so irresponsible as to constitute a danger to society, I do not believe that society can carefully preserve in existence the danger they represent. I believe that society is justified in destroying even the irresponsible murderer if he is known to imperil the life of other persons. There should be no sentiment about it. Persons whose existence means death and disaster to others who have done no wrong have no claim upon society for anything—not even for life itself.

Safety of Citizens

Nothing is more remarkable in the evolution of a community than the growing regard for human life. A community is held to be civilized, or not, in exact proportion to the safety of the common citizen. When the life of an individual is unjustly taken by another individual, the horror of the community for such an act cannot be adequately and proportionately manifested except as the community surmounts sentiment and exacts the life of the killer in payment—after a trial, where all opportunity of defense is accorded, and after all possible human excuses and palliations have been alleged, tested, and found insufficient.

R.L. Calder, "Is Capital Punishment Right? A Debate," *The Forum*, September 1928.

Few men who murder have previously lived blameless lives. The act of murder is the climax—a cumulative effect of countless previous thoughts and acts. The man's conduct depends upon his philosophy of life. Those who want to grow up to be respectable and useful citizens in the community have a correct philosophy. Those who want to excel in crime, those who tear down instead of building up, deliberately choose to adopt the wrong philosophy of life and to make their conduct correspond with it.

Society and particularly the state would not be much concerned with individual codes of conduct if, at the present time, they were not adopted by the youths of the land and were not creating an army of virtual anarchists who look upon the criminal code, including that part of it forbidding murder, as a mere convention of society which "advanced thinking" and crazy social theories permit them to set aside as a matter of no consequence.

Because some of the youth of our population are saturated with these ideas, we are asked to accept fantastic notions, abnormal actions, and even defiance, disregard, and violation of the law, as the reason for turning them loose when charged with murder. We are compelled to listen to the weirdest, wildest, and most fantastic theories expounded by expert witnesses to show why capital punishment should not be inflicted. . . .

If the United States of America has the power to take boys of eighteen years of age and send them to their death in the front line trenches in countries overseas in defense of our laws, I believe that the state has an equal right to take the lives of murderers of like age for violating the mandate of God and man, "Thou shalt not kill."

I base my belief that capital punishment is a deterrent of crime upon the fact that where capital punishment has been inflicted for even a comparatively small period and in a relatively small number of cases, there subsequently has been an immediate decrease in murder. Those who argue against capital punishment should bear in mind that where capital punishment has actually been inflicted, this has been the result. But, capital punishment has never been given a fair trial throughout this country over a sufficient period of time and in a sufficient number of cases to justify the assumption that it is not a deterrent of murder.

Until American society finds a way to protect itself from the murder of its members, this country will continue to be known as "the most lawless nation claiming place among the civilized nations of the world." I am not proud of that appellation. I hang my head in shame whenever I hear it. I believe society should have no hesitancy in springing the trap every time the noose can be put around a murderer's neck.

VIEWPOINT

"It is hardly probable that the great majority of people refrain from killing their neighbors because they are afraid; they refrain because they never had the inclination."

Capital Punishment Will Not Safeguard Society (1928)

Clarence Darrow

Clarence Darrow was a Chicago lawyer who became famous for his handling of criminal and labor cases. He chose to defend those whom he considered social unfortunates. He argued on behalf of more than one hundred people charged with murder, none of whom were sentenced to death. Although he retired in 1927, he continued to write prolifically on the causes of crime and to argue vehemently for the abolition of the death penalty. His most famous courtroom pleas are included in the book *Attorney for the Damned.* In the following viewpoint, Darrow maintains that capital punishment is no deterrent to crime. He advances his theory that as victims of their culture, criminals need to be treated more humanely.

As you read, consider the following questions:

1. To what does Darrow attribute the causes of crime, specifically murder?
2. What arguments does the author offer to support his belief that capital punishment is no deterrent to murder?

Clarence Darrow, "The Futility of the Death Penalty," *The Forum,* September 1928.

Little more than a century ago, in England, there were over two hundred offenses that were punishable with death. The death sentence was passed upon children under ten years old. And every time the sentimentalist sought to lessen the number of crimes punishable by death, the self-righteous said no, that it would be the destruction of the state; that it would be better to kill for more transgressions rather than for less.

Today, both in England and America, the number of capital offenses has been reduced to a very few, and capital punishment would doubtless be abolished altogether were it not for the self-righteous, who still defend it with the same old arguments. Their major claim is that capital punishment decreases the number of murders, and hence, that the state must retain the institution as its last defense against the criminal.

It is my purpose in this article to prove, first, that capital punishment is no deterrent to crime; and second, that the state continues to kill its victims, not so much to defend society against them—for it could do that equally well by imprisonment—but to appease the mob's emotions of hatred and revenge.

The Criminal Disease

Behind the idea of capital punishment lies false training and crude views of human conduct. People do evil things, say the judges, lawyers, and preachers, because of depraved hearts. Human conduct is not determined by the causes which determine the conduct of other animal and plant life in the universe. For some mysterious reason human beings act as they please; and if they do not please to act in a certain way, it is because, having the power of choice, they deliberately choose to act wrongly. The world once applied this doctrine to disease and insanity in men. It was also applied to animals, and even inanimate things were once tried and condemned to destruction. The world knows better now, but the rule has not yet been extended to human beings.

The simple fact is that every person starts life with a certain physical structure, more or less sensitive, stronger or weaker. He is played upon by everything that reaches him from without, and in this he is like everything else in the universe, inorganic matter as well as organic. How a man will act depends upon the character of his human machine, and the strength of the various stimuli that affect it. Everyone knows that this is so in disease and insanity. Most investigators know that it applies to crime. But the great mass of people still sit in judgment, robed with self-righteousness, and determine the fate of their less fortunate fellows. When this question is studied like any other, we shall then know how to get rid of most of the conduct that we call "criminal," just as we are now getting rid of much of the disease that once afflicted mankind.

If crime were really the result of willful depravity, we should be ready to concede that capital punishment may serve as a deterrent to the criminally inclined. But it is hardly probable that the great majority of people refrain from killing their neighbors because they are afraid; they refrain because they never had the inclination. Human beings are creatures of habit and, as a rule, they are not in the habit of killing. The circumstances that lead to killings are manifold, but in a particular individual the inducing cause is not easily found. In one case, homicide may have been induced by indigestion in the killer; in another, it may be traceable to some weakness inherited from a remote ancestor; but that it results from *something* tangible and understandable, if all the facts were known, must be plain to everyone who believes in cause and effect.

Of course, no one will be converted to this point of view by statistics of crime. In the first place, it is impossible to obtain reliable ones; and in the second place, the conditions to which they apply are never the same. But if one cares to analyze the figures, such as we have, it is easy to trace the more frequent causes of homicide. The greatest number of killings occur during attempted burglaries and robberies. The robber knows that penalties for burglary do not average more than five years in prison. He also knows that the penalty for murder is death or life imprisonment. Faced with this alternative, what does the burglar do when he is detected and threatened with arrest? He shoots to kill. He deliberately takes the chance of death to save himself from a five-year term in prison. It is therefore as obvious as anything can be that fear of death has no effect in diminishing homicides of this kind, which are more numerous than any other type.

The next largest number of homicides may be classed as "sex murders." Quarrels between husbands and wives, disappointed love, or love too much requited cause many killings. They are the result of primal emotions so deep that the fear of death has not the slightest effect in preventing them. Spontaneous feelings overflow in criminal acts, and consequences do not count. Then there are cases of sudden anger, uncontrollable rage. The fear of death never enters into such cases; if the anger is strong enough, consequences are not considered until too late. The old-fashioned stories of men deliberately plotting and committing murder in cold blood have little foundation in real life. Such killings are so rare that they need not concern us here. The point to be emphasized is that practically all homicides are manifestations of well-recognized human emotions, and it is perfectly plain that the fear of excessive punishment does not enter into them.

Punishment Is No Cure for Crime

There is no deterrent in the menace of the gallows.

Cruelty and viciousness are not abolished by cruelty and viciousness—not even by legalized cruelty and viciousness. . . .

Our penal system has broken down because it is built upon the sand—founded on the basis of force and violence—instead of on the basis of Christian care of our fellow men, of moral and mental human development, of the conscientious performance by the State of its duty to the citizen.

We cannot cure murder by murder.

We must adopt another and better system.

William Randolph Hearst, *The Congressional Digest*, August/September 1927.

In addition to these personal forces which overwhelm weak men and lead them to commit murder, there are also many social and economic forces which must be listed among the causes of homicides, and human beings have even less control over these than over their own emotions. It is often said that in America there are more homicides in proportion to population than in England. This is true. There are likewise more in the United States than in Canada. But such comparisons are meaningless until one takes into consideration the social and economic differences in the countries compared. Then it becomes apparent why the homicide rate in the United States is higher. Canada's population is largely rural; that of the United States is crowded into cities whose slums are the natural breeding places of crime. Moreover, the population of England and Canada is homogeneous, while the United States has gathered together people of every color from every nation in the world. Racial differences intensify social, religious, and industrial problems, and the confusion which attends this indiscriminate mixing of races and nationalities is one of the most fertile sources of crime.

Primitive Beliefs

Will capital punishment remedy these conditions? Of course it won't; but its advocates argue that the fear of this extreme penalty will hold the victims of adverse conditions in check. To this piece of sophistry the continuance and increase of crime in our large cities is a sufficient answer. No, the plea that capital punishment acts as a deterrent to crime will not stand. The real reason why this barbarous practice persists in a so-called civilized world is that people still hold the primitive belief that the taking of one human life can be atoned for by taking another. It is the age-old obsession with punishment that keeps the official headsman busy plying his trade.

And it is precisely upon this point that I would build my case against capital punishment. Even if one grants that the idea of punishment is sound, crime calls for something more—for careful study, for an understanding of causes, for proper remedies. To attempt to abolish crime by killing the criminal is the easy and foolish way out of a serious situation. Unless a remedy deals with the conditions which foster crime, criminals will breed faster than the hangman can spring his trap. Capital punishment ignores the causes of crime just as completely as the primitive witch doctor ignored the causes of disease; and, like the methods of the witch doctor, it is not only ineffective as a remedy, but is positively vicious in at least two ways. In the first place, the spectacle of state executions feeds the basest passions of the mob. And in the second place, so long as the state rests content to deal with crime in this barbaric and futile manner, society will be lulled by a false sense of security, and effective methods of dealing with crime will be discouraged. . . .

Crime in England

For the last five or six years, in England and Wales, the homicides reported by the police range from sixty-five to seventy a year. Death sentences meted out by jurors have averaged about thirty-five, and hangings, fifteen. More than half of those convicted by juries were saved by appeals to the Home Office. But in America there is no such percentage of lives saved after conviction. Governors are afraid to grant clemency. If they did, the newspapers and the populace would refuse to reelect them.

Failure to Instill Fear

It is a fact that a large percentage of murders are committed in the heat of passion, when the murderer is not in a position to reason; fear of the law plays no part at all. In the remaining few, whatever fear there may be is more than balanced by the belief on the part of the criminal that he is not going to get caught. There are also some who deliberately kill; but the knowledge that they will be caught and punished does not deter them.

Thomas Mott Osborne, "Thou Shalt Not Kill," *The Forum*, February 1925.

It is true that trials are somewhat prompter in England than America, but there no newspaper dares publish the details of any case until after the trial. In America the accused is often convicted by the public within twenty-four hours of the time a homicide occurs. The courts sidetrack all other business so that a homicide that is widely discussed may receive prompt attention. The road to the gallows is not only opened but greased for the opportunity of killing another victim. . . .

Human conduct is by no means so simple as our moralists have led us to believe. There is no sharp line separating good actions from bad. The greed for money, the display of wealth, the despair of those who witness the display, the poverty, oppression, and hopelessness of the unfortunate—all these are factors which enter into human conduct and of which the world takes no account. Many people have learned no other profession but robbery and burglary. The processions moving steadily through our prisons to the gallows are in the main made up of these unfortunates. And how do we dare to consider ourselves civilized creatures when, ignoring the causes of crime, we rest content to mete out harsh punishments to the victims of conditions over which they have no control?

Even now, are not all imaginative and humane people shocked at the spectacle of a killing by the state? How many men and women would be willing to act as executioners? How many fathers and mothers would want their children to witness an official killing? What kind of people read the sensational reports of an execution? If all right-thinking men and women were not ashamed of it, why would it be needful that judges and lawyers and preachers apologize for the barbarity? How can the state censure the cruelty of the man who—moved by strong passions, or acting to save his freedom, or influenced by weakness or fear—takes human life, when everyone knows that the state itself, after long premeditation and settled hatred, not only kills, but first tortures and bedevils its victims for weeks with the impending doom?

More Humane Criminal Code

For the last hundred years the world has shown a gradual tendency to mitigate punishment. We are slowly learning that this way of controlling human beings is both cruel and ineffective. In England the criminal code has consistently grown more humane, until now the offenses punishable by death are reduced to practically one. If there is any reason for singling out this one, neither facts nor philosophy can possibly demonstrate it. There is no doubt whatever that the world is growing more humane and more sensitive and more understanding. The time will come when all people will view with horror the light way in which society and its courts of law now take human life; and when that time comes, the way will be clear to devise some better method of dealing with poverty and ignorance and their frequent by-products which we call crime.

CHAPTER 2

Is the Death Penalty Just?

Chapter Preface

In 1968, executions were suspended in the United States while the courts debated the legitimacy of capital punishment. After the 1972 case of *Furman v. Georgia*, the U.S. Supreme Court ruled that the application of the death penalty in thirty-five states was unconstitutional. This decision resulted in significant reforms to capital punishment at the state level, including a ban on mandatory death penalties, restricting capital punishment to the crime of murder, and obligatory appeals for death sentences. The Supreme Court then reinstated the death penalty in 1976, enabling states to resume executions in 1977. During the 1980s and 1990s the rise in violent crime apparently bolstered popular support for capital punishment. Since the mid-1990s, 60 to 75 percent of the American public has favored the death penalty—many maintaining that it is the most just punishment for the crime of murder.

Supporters of capital punishment often contend that it is the only appropriate response to felony homicide. They believe that true justice requires a murderer to face a punishment that is comparable to the damage caused by his crime. As columnist David Leibowitz explains, "In a nation where justice is often represented by a set of scales, execution as punishment for a depraved murder marks the ultimate—and only—systemic balance." Moreover, proponents argue, capital punishment affirms society's moral recognition that some crimes are not to be tolerated.

Critics, however, often contend that deliberate killing—by either a criminal or by the state—is ethically unacceptable. While they grant that murderers should receive severe punishment, they believe that the state undermines its moral authority when it executes killers to proclaim that murder is wrong. As explained in a statement drafted by the Catholic Deacons of Paterson, New Jersey, "Increasingly, our society looks to violent measures to deal with some of our most difficult social problems . . . including increased reliance on the death penalty. . . . Violence is not the solution: It is the most clear sign of our failures. . . . We cannot teach that killing is wrong by killing." State-sanctioned execution, they maintain, ultimately denies the intrinsic value of each human life.

With the recent calls for additional reforms in the administration of the death penalty, the debate over the morality of executions will likely grow more complex in the years to come. The authors in the following chapter present several arguments concerning the logic and ethics of capital punishment.

VIEWPOINT 1

"We simply do not believe that premeditated, state-sanctioned killing is justifiable under any circumstances."

The Death Penalty Is Unjust

Progressive

State-supported execution—even for the most brutal murderers—is ethically wrong and can never be justified, contend the editors of the *Progressive* in the following viewpoint. Capital punishment is physically and psychologically cruel and is disproportionately administered to minorities and the poor, the authors point out. Moreover, innocent and wrongly convicted inmates might have already been executed. The death penalty should be abolished because it brutalizes society and denies the value of human life. The *Progressive* is a monthly journal of left-wing political opinion.

As you read, consider the following questions:

1. According to the authors, why did the U.S. Supreme Court agree to review Florida's use of the electric chair?
2. According to Helen Prejean, quoted by the authors, what is torturous about the practice of capital punishment?
3. What flaws did *Chicago Tribune* reporters uncover in their investigation of capital punishment in Illinois?

Reprinted, with permission, from "The Case Against the Death Penalty," editorial, *The Progressive*, February 2000.

In December 1999, a convicted killer in Texas named David Long attempted suicide by overdosing on antipsychotic medication shortly before he was to be executed. He was placed on life support and revived, then removed from the hospital against the advice of his doctor. "Placed in intensive care on a ventilator in a Galveston hospital, Mr. Long suddenly presented a politically delicate question for [then] Governor George W. Bush, even as he campaigned for the Republican Presidential nomination in New Hampshire," said the *New York Times*. "Would the state of Texas remove an inmate from intensive care so that he could meet his date with his executioner rather than stay the execution for thirty days? The answer is yes."

The case of David Long tops a long list of bizarre and indecent instances of capital punishment in 1999. It was a year for the executioner. Ninety-eight were put to death, the most since states began to dust off the death machinery in 1976.

In Texas, George W. Bush presided over thirty-five executions in 1999, the most of any state in the country. This brings the total during his tenure as governor to 112. He has granted one act of clemency in that time. During the election year (2000), George W. has plenty of company on the campaign circuit. Every Republican and Democratic candidate for President supports the death penalty. But Bush may be the most gung-ho. He beat Ann Richards in the 1994 campaign for governor by attacking her execution record as slow. Richards had allowed fifty executions during the four years she held office. Easily besting her, Bush has limited the ability of prisoners to appeal their death sentences. In the spring of 1999, as he began his campaign for President of the United States, he opposed a state bill that would have banned the use of capital punishment on those who are mentally retarded. The bill failed.

At times, Bush seems insensitive to the plight of the people he is sending to the death chamber. In an interview with *Talk* magazine in the summer of 1999, he mocked convicted double murderer Karla Faye Tucker for her last-minute mercy plea.

We at the *Progressive* have a long history of opposing capital punishment on moral grounds. We believe every human being deserves the dignity of life. This includes the most brutal of murderers. We simply do not believe that premeditated, state-sanctioned killing is justifiable under any circumstances. The death penalty brutalizes us. It is an indication of how little our government values human life.

But the case against the death penalty does not rest solely on this pillar. Capital punishment is cruel, both physically and psychologically. People have been executed who very well might have been innocent. The death penalty is not applied consistently. And it discriminates against minorities and the poor.

As to cruelty, there can be no question. In 1997, Pedro Medina's head caught fire while he was being electrocuted in Florida. State Attorney General Bob Butterworth commented, "People who wish to commit murder, they better not do it in the state of Florida, because we may have a problem with our electric chair." In 1999, that state had another botched execution: In June, Allen Lee Davis started to bleed profusely from the nose and appeared to suffer extreme pain during electrocution. After the machine was turned off, he continued to breathe. "Witnesses say his chest rose and fell about ten times before he went still," reported the *New York Times*. The occurrence prompted the Supreme Court to agree to review Florida's use of the electric chair, and Florida's state legislature has offered lethal injection as an alternative.

Although the electric chair is gruesome, other methods of execution currently practiced in the United States—particularly hanging and the gas chamber—are capable of producing excruciating pain, as well.

Sister Helen Prejean, who was portrayed by Susan Sarandon in the movie *Dead Man Walking*, counsels death row convicts in the Louisiana State Penitentiary at Angola. She has seen the psychological cruelty of death row. "People may be able to control their consciousness, but they can't control their dreams," she said at the November 1998 First National Conference on Death and Dying in Prisons and Jails (sponsored by the Open Society Institute). "Everybody I have known on death row always had the same nightmare: 'They're coming for me, they're dragging me out of my cell, they're bringing me to the execution chamber. I'm fighting,

I'm screaming, No, no! And then I wake up and I'm in a sweat. And then I realize, oh, no, it's not my time yet.'"

It is this psychological aspect of capital punishment that leads Prejean to call it a "practice of torture." "We don't torture people physically by flogging them in the public square until they bleed to death," she said. "But the reason that you can't take the torture out of the death penalty is that conscious human beings condemned to death anticipate death, have imaginations, and die a thousand times before they die."

The Danger of Wrongful Convictions

The death penalty, once applied, is irrevocable. And the record of false convictions for those who end up on death row provides no reassurance that innocent people are not being executed. In 1999, eight people were freed and declared innocent of their crimes, bringing the total of those exonerated from death row to eighty-four since 1973, or about one-seventh of all those executed. These inmates had spent an average of 7.5 years on death row before winning release because evidence of their innocence emerged—an eloquent testament to the dangers of quicker executions.

A recent *Chicago Tribune* investigation found that at least 381 homicide convictions across the country have been overturned since 1963 because prosecutors were discovered to have concealed evidence of innocence or because they used evidence they knew to be false. None of these prosecutors, said the investigation, has been disbarred or convicted.

"Just how often the police actually get the wrong man is nothing short of astounding," says an article in the November 1999 issue of the *Atlantic Monthly*. "A 1996 Justice Department report *Convicted by Juries, Exonerated by Science: Case Studies in the Use of DNA Evidence to Establish Innocence After Trial* found that in 8,048 rape and rape-and-murder cases referred to the FBI crime lab from 1988 to mid-1995, a staggering 2,012 of the primary suspects were exonerated owing to DNA evidence alone."

Unfair Application of the Death Penalty

The death penalty is hardly applied evenhandedly across the country. Two people can commit the same offense but receive very different treatment, depending on where they live. "Death penalty conviction rates can vary dramatically between neighboring counties imposing identical state laws," reported *USA Today*. And the percentage of executions in the South (80 percent) as opposed to the rest of the country (11 percent in the Midwest, 8 percent in the West, and 0.5 percent in the Northeast) is striking evidence of the geographical distortions that mark executions in the United States. According to data from the Death Penalty Information Center, in 1999, Connecticut had five people on death row, Kansas had two, while Texas had 443.

In 1994, just before he retired, Justice Harry Blackmun, who had supported the death penalty for decades, turned against it precisely because it was administered so inconsistently. "I no longer shall tinker with the machinery of death," he wrote.

African Americans make up 12 percent of the population of the United States but account for 35 percent of those currently on death row. "A 1998 University of Iowa study of sentencing in Philadelphia showed that the odds of receiving a death sentence are nearly 3.9 times greater if the defendant is black," reports the Death Penalty Information Center.

But the death penalty is more closely linked to the race of the victim. A 1998 report by the Death Penalty Information Center found that in Florida, "a defendant's odds of receiving a death sentence are 4.8 times higher if the victim was white than if the victim was black in similarly aggravated cases. In Illinois, the multiplier is 4, in Oklahoma, it is 4.3, in North Carolina, 4.4, and in Mississippi, it is 5.5. . . . The state of Kentucky presents a particularly outrageous example of race-of-victim discrimination: Despite the fact that 1,000 African Americans have been murdered there since the 1975 reinstitution of the death penalty in that state, as of spring 1999, all of the state's thirty-nine death row inmates were sentenced for murdering a white victim; none were there for murdering a black victim."

Death row is a ghetto of poor people. "The average capital defendant doesn't have the money to hire O.J. Simpson's 'dream team,'" reported the *Atlantic*. "More likely than not, he has no money at all. At the very least, three-fourths of state prison inmates and half of federal prison inmates have taxpayer-financed court-appointed counsel. The quality of this representation is questionable."

When it comes to the constitutional right to representation, the situation for defendants in capital cases is dismal. "Eighteen death penalty states lack statewide public defender organizations, and many of those that have them underfund them so seriously that lawyers end up handling huge caseloads that would be considered unconscionable, to say nothing of impractical, in the private sector," said the *Atlantic*.

Revenge Does Not Justify Killing

Beneath the usual justifications for punishing criminals lurks a more visceral and potent motive for the death penalty: revenge. The desire to lash back at those who have harmed us has deep roots in our evolutionary past. It is a powerful human motive that must be taken seriously, but it is not a sufficient justification for killing. Although individually we all feel the primitive urge to exact revenge against those who harm us, collectively we must strive to be more rational, fair, moral, and humane than the criminals who commit the acts of violence or cruelty that we condemn.

Mark Costanzo, *Just Revenge: Costs and Consequences of the Death Penalty*, 1997.

Some who have been executed were juveniles at the time they committed their crimes or had severe mental disabilities. Amnesty International has been sharply critical of all countries, but particularly the United States, for the practice of sentencing such individuals to death.

"International human rights treaties prohibit anyone under eighteen years old at the time of the crime being sentenced to death," says Amnesty International. "Nevertheless, five countries since 1990 are known to have executed prisoners who were under eighteen years old at the time of the crime: Iran, Pakistan, Saudi Arabia, the U.S.A., and Yemen. The majority of known executions of juveniles has been in the U.S.A." The United States has executed ten since 1990. Seventy youth offenders are currently on death row. Nearly one-third of these are in Texas.

When death row prisoners are freed, often it occurs not

because the legal system is fail-safe but because dedicated lawyers, journalists, activists, scholars, and students have brought the injustice out into the light of day.

David Protess, a professor of journalism at Northwestern University, has his students look into questionable convictions. Altogether, he and his students have managed to free five inmates from Illinois prisons. Three were on death row. The most recent of these, Anthony Porter, came within two days of execution. "It would certainly be hard to conclude that the death penalty is working when eighty-four people have been freed from death row in the last twenty-five years," says Protess. "This is not a conservative or liberal issue. The machinery of death is broken and it cannot be fixed."

In November 1999, reporters at the *Chicago Tribune* examined all the death penalty convictions in Illinois in the twenty-two years since capital punishment was reinstated—285 altogether. "Capital punishment in Illinois is a system so riddled with faulty evidence, unscrupulous trial tactics, and legal incompetence that justice has been forsaken," the reporters declared in summing up their discoveries.

Here's what they found:

- At least forty-six times, evidence against the defendant included a jailhouse snitch—a notoriously unreliable form of testimony.
- At least twenty times, evidence involved a visual comparison of body hair, a type of forensic science known to be imprecise and subjective.
- In at least thirty-three cases, the defending attorney had been, or was later, suspended or disbarred.
- In at least thirty-five cases, "a defendant sent to death row was black and the jury that determined guilt or sentence was all white."
- Eight death row inmates were allegedly tortured by former commander Jon Burge of the Chicago Police Department and several detectives under his direction. "Among the accusations leveled at the Burge regime are that detectives beat suspects, shocked them with electric wires, and put guns to their mouths in order to get confessions," the report notes. In 1993, Burge was fired because he had allegedly tortured an inmate during an investigation. When the *Tribune*

reporters contacted Burge, he declined to comment.

• In some cases, many of these improprieties appear in a single case. "Dennis Williams, who is black, was sentenced to die by an all white Cook County jury, prosecuted with evidence that included a jailhouse informant, and defended—none too well—by an attorney who was later disbarred." He was subsequently freed as the result of evidence uncovered by Protess's class.

Protess believes Illinois may have a better record than other states. "We're catching the errors before it's too late," he says. "But it's important to point out that this is the result of pressure from outside—religious leaders, journalists, and college students, as opposed to the system correcting itself. We can't count on the system to fix this problem. It has to be pressured."

Exploiting Capital Punishment

Meanwhile, there are plenty of politicians ready to exploit capital punishment.

"Kirk Fordice promised in his campaign that he would make Mississippi the 'capital of capital punishment,'" the *Atlantic* reported. "Kentucky Governor Paul Patton signed five execution warrants on his second day in office, though all five cases were still pending in court. Bob Martinez has bragged that he signed some ninety death warrants during his four years as governor of Florida. And Governor Bill Clinton flew to Arkansas during the 1992 New Hampshire Presidential primary for the execution of a brain-damaged man who had killed a policeman. Flouting Supreme Court rulings against executing the mentally incompetent, Clinton seized control of the crime issue for the Democratic Party."

The average length of time spent on death row decreased by three months in 1998. But opportunistic politicians have vowed to decrease it further. George W. Bush succeeded in doing so in Texas. In January 2000, Florida Governor Jeb Bush convened a special three-day legislative session to pass laws cutting the time between sentencing and execution. The resulting law is intended to reduce the average time on death row to five years—down from a current average of fourteen. In Virginia, those convicted of murder have just twenty-one days to introduce new evidence of their innocence. Laws like the 1996 Anti-Terrorism and Effective Death Penalty Act, which makes it more difficult for convicts to obtain federal review of claims that their constitutional rights have been violated, are also designed to hasten the march to the death chamber.

Criticism of the Death Penalty

A burgeoning global movement is harshly critical of the United States on the issue of the death penalty. The European Union has called on the United States to end the practice. So, too, has the Inter-American Court on Human Rights. And Amnesty International launched an unprecedented campaign against the United States because of its use of capital punishment.

U.S. religious leaders also have taken a strong stand. "We oppose capital punishment not just for what it does to those guilty of horrible crimes, but for what it does to all of us as a society," says a March 1999 joint statement by U.S. Jewish and Catholic leaders. "Increasing reliance on the death penalty diminishes all of us and is a sign of growing disrespect for human life. We cannot overcome crime by simply executing criminals, nor can we restore the lives of the innocent by ending the lives of those convicted of their murders. The death penalty offers the tragic illusion that we defend life by taking life." And the Pope has called for international abolition of capital punishment to mark the new millennium.

This movement has found at least one ally in the U.S. Senate. In mid-November 1999, Senator Russ Feingold, Democrat of Wisconsin, introduced a bill to abolish the federal death penalty and called on all states to cease the practice.

"We are a nation that prides itself on the fundamental principles of justice, liberty, equality, and due process," Feingold said in announcing his bill. "We are one of the first nations to speak out against torture and killings by foreign governments. It is time for us to look in the mirror."

In the 1972 case *Furman v. Georgia*, the Supreme Court struck down the death penalty, declaring among other things that it had been applied arbitrarily and used unfairly against the poor and African Americans. In a concurring opinion, Justice Thurgood Marshall attacked capital punishment in these words: "It is excessive, unnecessary, and offensive to contemporary values." The Supreme Court should take another close look at this barbaric practice and end the death race once and for all.

Many of those on death row may no longer be threats to society. Some, no doubt, may be. But for those who are, there are options less cruel and unusual that do not put society at risk. Life without parole is one. A lengthy sentence with treatment, with release conditional upon proof of rehabilitation, is another.

But our political leaders do not want to consider these options. Instead, they pander to the basest, most vengeful impulses of the public.

For Prejean, the issue is simple. Accompanying someone to execution "focuses everything for you. Where are you? What side are you on? Are you for life or are you for death? Are you for compassion or are you for vengeance?" she said. "Because there is no way you can take the death penalty and call it anything else other than an act of distilled hatred."

2

VIEWPOINT

"[Murder] is final. So is the death penalty, which, therefore, traditionally has been thought fitting."

The Death Penalty Is Just

Ernest van den Haag

The death penalty is just, argues Ernest van den Haag in the following viewpoint. He contends that human beings are morally responsible for their actions and should therefore be punished accordingly for their crimes. In the case of murder, a death sentence is appropriate because it punishes the criminal in proportion to the harm caused by his crime. Furthermore, the author asserts, any unfair or wrongful application of capital punishment does not warrant abolishing the practice. Justice is still justice even if it is administered unfairly. Ultimately, retributive justice should be informed—but not replaced—by mercy, he concludes. Van den Haag is a psychoanalyst and retired professor of jurisprudence and public policy.

As you read, consider the following questions:

1. In van den Haag's opinion, what is the primary moral purpose of punishment?
2. What are the non-moral purposes of punishment, according to the author?
3. In the author's view, why is it better to risk executing some innocent people than to abandon capital punishment?

Traditionally murder has been thought the most grave of crimes, deserving the most severe punishment. Other crimes, such as theft, or even rape, leave the victim capable of recovering. Murder does not. It is final. So is the death penalty, which, therefore, traditionally has been thought fitting.

Can any crime be horrible enough to forfeit the life of the criminal? Can death ever be a deserved punishment? Some abolitionists do not think so. Others even believe, for unintelligible reasons, that no society has a moral right to impose the death penalty. I am confident that the following excerpt may help answer this question.

> . . . The appellant, after telling Donna how pretty she was, raised his fist and hit her across the face. When she stood up, he grabbed her by her blouse, ripping it off. He then proceeded to remove her bra and tied her hands behind her back with a nylon stocking. McCorquodale then removed his belt, which was fastened with a rather large buckle, and repeatedly struck Donna across the back with the buckle end of the belt. He then took off all her clothing and then bound her mouth with tape and a washcloth. Leroy then kicked Donna and she fell to the floor. McCorquodale took his cigarette and burned the victim on the breasts, the thigh, and the navel. He then bit one of Donna's nipples and she began to bleed. He asked for a razorblade and then sliced the other nipple. He then called for a box of salt and poured it into the wounds he had made on her breasts. At this point Linda, who was eight months pregnant, became ill and went into the bedroom and closed the door. McCorquodale then lit a candle and proceeded to drip hot wax over Donna's body. He held the candle about 1/2 inch from Donna's vagina and dripped the hot wax into this part of her body. He then used a pair of surgical scissors to cut around the victim's clitoris.
>
> While bleeding from her nose and vagina, Leroy forced the victim to perform oral sex on him while McCorquodale had intercourse with her. Then Leroy had intercourse with the victim while McCorquodale forced his penis into the victim's mouth. McCorquodale then found a hard plastic bottle which was about 5 inches in height and placed an antiseptic solution within it, forcing this bottle into Donna's vagina and squirted the solution into her. The victim was then permitted to go to the bathroom to "get cleaned up." While she was in the bathroom, McCorquodale secured a piece of nylon rope and told Bonnie and her roommate that he was going "to kill the girl." He hid in a closet across the hall from the bathroom and when Donna came out of the bathroom he

wrapped the nylon cord around her neck. Donna screamed, "My God, you're killing me." As McCorquodale tried to strangle her, the cord cut into his hands and Donna fell to the floor. He fell on top of her and began to strangle her with his bare hands. He removed his hands and the victim began to have convulsions. He again strangled her and then pulled her head up and forward to break her neck. He covered her lifeless body with a sheet and departed the apartment to search for a means of transporting her body from the scene. By this time, it was approximately 6:00 a.m. on the morning of January 17.

McCorquodale soon returned to the apartment and asked Bonnie for her trunk and Leroy and McCorquodale tried to place Donna's body in the trunk. Finding that the body was too large for the trunk McCorquodale proceeded to break Donna's arms and legs by holding them upright while he stomped on them with his foot. Donna's body was then placed in the trunk and the trunk was placed in the closet behind the curtains. McCorquodale and Leroy then went to sleep on the couch in the living room for the greater portion of the day, leaving the apartment sometime during the afternoon.

Because a strong odor began to emanate from the body, and her efforts to mask the smell with deodorant spray had been unsuccessful, Linda called Bonnie to request that McCorquodale remove the trunk from the apartment. Shortly after 8:00 p.m. McCorquodale arrived at the apartment with a person named Larry. As they attempted to move the trunk from the closet, blood began spilling from the trunk onto the living room floor. McCorquodale placed a towel under the trunk to absorb the blood as they carried the trunk to Larry's car. When McCorquodale and Larry returned to the apartment they told Linda that the body had been dumped out of the trunk into a road and that the trunk was placed under some boxes in a "Dempsey Dumpster." Donna's body was found about half a mile off Highway No. 42 in Clayton County. (*McCorquodale v. State* 1974:579–580)

Murder Deserves Blame

Justice William Brennan thought the death penalty inconsistent with "the sanctity of life." His unargued notion may derive from the ancient *homo homini res sacra* (man is a sacred object to man). But the Romans, who coined the phrase, believed the sanctity of life best safeguarded by executing murderers who had not respected it. Brennan may also have based his view on the Constitution. However, it does not grant an imprescriptible right to life which murderers would be as entitled to as their victims. He also held that execution is a "denial of the executed person's humanity." Yet, philosophers, such as Immanuel Kant and G.W.F. Hegel, thought that punishments, including the death penalty, recognize and asseverate the humanity of the convict, even though he himself may have repudiated it by his crime.

We protect ourselves from ferocious beasts, but we do not punish them, because, unlike criminals, they cannot tell right from wrong or restrain themselves accordingly. Animals therefore are not, but criminals are responsible for their actions because they are human. Their punishment acknowledges rather than denies their responsibility and, thereby, their humanity. Brennan finally asserts that "the deliberate extinguishment of human life by the state is uniquely degrading to human dignity." He does not tell whether the criminal or the executioner is degraded, nor wherein the degradation lies, or whether any crime could degrade humanity and call for a degrading punishment.

Capital punishment, a deliberate expulsion from human society, is meant to add deserved moral ignominy to death. This irks some abolitionists, who feel that nobody should be blamed for whatever he does. But murder deserves blame. Death may well be less punishment than what some criminals deserve. Even torture may be. But, although they may deserve it, we no longer torture criminals. Unlike death, torture is avoidable. It is now repulsive to most people, and no longer thought entertaining, as it was in the past. . . .

The Purpose of Punishment

The paramount moral purpose of punishment is retributive justice. But there are important non-moral purposes as well, such as protection of life and property. They are achieved mainly by deterrence. It seems obvious that more severe and certain punishments deter more than less severe and certain ones. Yet, abolitionists contend that the death penalty is no more deterrent than life in prison, or, alternatively, that the additional deterrence is redundant. As mentioned, this empirical question could be decided by experiment. We could threaten capital punishment for murders committed on Mondays, Wednesdays, and Fridays (MWF) and life imprisonment on the other days. If fewer murders are committed on MWF, the death penalty would be likely to be more deterrent than life in prison. However, the MWF murders do not deserve more punishment than the others. It would be morally capricious to impose the death penalty just on MWF murderers. We will have to rely on observation and statistical analysis, rather than experiment, to establish degrees of deterrence. Preponderantly, though not conclusively, the data tend to show the death penalty to be the most deterrent punishment available. Possibly, people fear the death penalty irrationally, despite low probability (executions are rare), just as they are irrationally attracted to lotteries with high prizes despite the low probability of winning.

The Moral Defense of the Death Penalty

Justice is a punitive response to a criminal that penalizes him in direct proportion to the harm he has done to actual individuals; to reflect back onto him the negative consequences of his criminal actions. . . .

The moral defense of the death penalty is the principle of justice. In the case of premeditated murder, capital punishment is the only just punishment: it is the only punishment roughly proportionate to the harm that has been done to the murder victim.

Now, anyone who respects life is understandably uneasy about taking even the lives of killers. But the principle of justice demands it, because proportionate punishment for crimes is the moral keystone of any system of justice.

Robert James Bidinotto, *LEAA Advocate*, Summer/Fall 1997.

Apart from less deterrence, life imprisonment, the alternative to capital punishment, also protects society less than capital punishment does. The convict may escape, he may be granted a furlough, or his sentence may be commuted by governors who, unavoidably, retain the right to pardon. Not least, the lifer may endanger guards and fellow prisoners, since without the death penalty there is no further punishment to deter him.

To proponents of capital punishment, deterrence, though

important, is not decisive. Justice is. Still, most believe that the threat of execution does deter more than life imprisonment. In contrast, abolitionists believe that capital punishment not only is morally unjustifiable, but also has no more deterrent effect than life imprisonment. However, they would continue to advocate abolition, even if the death penalty were shown to deter more than life imprisonment. In effect, abolitionists appear to believe that the non-execution of murderers is morally more important than saving the innocent lives execution would save if it deters more than imprisonment. Asked whether they would execute murderers if each execution were to deter ten murders, thereby saving ten innocent lives, all abolitionists I have questioned answer in the negative. . . .

The Question of Innocents

If an innocent is executed the miscarriage of justice is irreparable. Since judges and juries are human and therefore fallible, we can minimize, but not altogether avoid such miscarriages. There is a trade-off in minimizing them. To avoid convicting innocents we require so much evidence for conviction that many guilty persons escape punishment—which is no less unjust than convicting the innocent. Guilt must be shown "beyond a reasonable doubt" and jurors must be unanimous. Courts exclude evidence and testimony if obtained unlawfully, e.g., by a search without a warrant, or without probable cause. This exclusion does not help in determining a defendant's guilt or innocence. There are many such exclusionary rules. They prevent courts from admitting much of the available evidence. They are meant to restrain the police. They may. But the exclusionary rules also help the guilty, when proof of their guilt cannot be admitted. Yet these rules do not protect the innocent who cannot benefit from the exclusion of evidence for guilt.

We have more than 20,000 homicides annually, but only about 300 death sentences (and less than 50 executions). At this rate most of the about 3,000 murderers now on death row are far more likely to die of old age than by execution. On the average convicts spend more than eight years appealing their convictions. This seems a long time. Many appeals are repetitious as well as frivolous. Despite elaborate precautions, nothing short of abolishing punishment can avoid miscarriages altogether. The salient question about the death penalty is not: Could innocents be executed by mistake? (The answer is yes—courts are fallible) but: Does the death penalty save more innocent lives than it takes? Is there a net gain or loss?

Many desirable social practices cannot avoid killing innocents by accident. For instance, ambulances save many lives, but also run over some pedestrians. We do not abolish ambulances, because they save more innocents than they kill. So does the death penalty, if it deters some murders, as is likely, and if the miscarriages are few, as is likely too. It seems safer then, to rely on executions, which through deterrence, may save innocent lives, than it would be not to execute and risk not saving an indefinite number of innocents who could have been saved. If we execute a convicted murderer and his execution does not produce additional deterrence, his execution, though just, would not have been useful. But if his execution deters prospective murderers, not executing him would sacrifice innocent people who would have been spared had he been executed. . . .

Unequal Justice Is Still Justice

Many abolitionists contend that the death penalty is distributed unfairly, that Blacks and the poor are likely to be executed for murders which are punished less severely when committed by whites. This was quite true at one time but recent data indicate it no longer is.

An unfair distribution of punishments (or rewards) is objectionable qua unfair. But it does not affect the moral quality of what is distributed. No objection to distribution does. Thus, if capital punishment is immoral per se even an impeccably fair distribution among the guilty would not justify it morally. On the other hand, if capital punishment is morally justified, no distribution, fair or unfair, could make it immoral.

Consider two kinds of discrimination. The death penalty (or any other punishment) may be distributed capriciously, e.g., by a lottery, among those equally guilty. The capriciousness cannot be avoided altogether. Criminal justice systems can minimize but not eliminate chance: one murderer may be found "not guilty" for lack of evidence. Another may be less lucky—even though both are equally guilty. Or, the discrimination may be intentional: the death penalty is deliberately imposed only, or mainly, on guilty Black murderers, never on legitimately guilty white ones. Such a distribution would be unfair and inconsistent with equal justice under law. But an unfair distribution does not affect the moral quality of what it distributes—unless the unfair distribution somehow inheres in the penalty and cannot be separated from it. Otherwise the moral quality of capital punishment is not more affected by its distribution than an unfair distribution of cookies affects their quality.

Although often conflated and confused, equality and justice are different concepts. Equal justice certainly does not mean equal equality. Rather, it means justice distributed according only to factors the law recognizes as relevant, i.e., independently of irrelevant factors such as wealth, race, or religion and independently of how the available evidence has been obtained.

We can have equal injustice. A tyrant may impose the death penalty on all his opponents, or on all Jews, bachelors, Bosnians or homosexuals. The distribution would be equal but the law, including the penalty, would be unjust. Equal injustice of this sort has occurred throughout history. So has unequal justice. No society has found a way to avoid inequality altogether though much progress has been made in avoiding deliberate inequality and discrimination. Still, accidental inequality, luck and chance play a greater role than we like. One guilty criminal will be convicted and executed while another gets away with murder. He was never caught, or the evidence left the court doubtful. Courts seek truth; but, at best, they find evidence. Yet, unequal justice is justice still and the best we can do. If Smith gets way with murder and Jones, guilty, but no more guilty than Smith, is executed Jones's guilt was not diminished. Guilt is personal. No murderer's guilt is diminished because other murderers escape punishment. It is objectionable that some murderers get away with impunity, but their impunity does not reduce the guilt of others. Justice demands that those deserving it suffer the death penalty, even if others, who deserve it no less, escape because of discrimination, prosecutorial incompetence, insufficient evidence or for any other reason.

David Baldus has investigated death sentences in Georgia to find that, if the victim of a Black murderer is white, the murderer is much more likely to be sentenced to death than if his victim had been Black. This practice clearly discriminates against Black victims whose life is valued less than that of white victims. The practice does not, however, discriminate against Black murderers. Indeed Black murderers are favored: murder tends to be intraracial; most black murderers murder black victims. Usually they are spared the death penalty, while white murderers, who murder white victims, are not.

Revenge Is Irrelevant

Punishments retribute for the harm, the disruption of peace and security, that crime imposes on society as well as for the harm done to individual victims. These victims may feel that retribution does (or does not) satisfy their wish for revenge. But retribution is independent of revenge even if often confused with it. Abolitionists, by identifying retribution with revenge, expect to benefit from the bad reputation revenge has acquired, which may go back to dubious interpretations of the Bible. In Romans XII:19 the apostle Paul writes: "Avenge not yourselves for . . . vengeance is mine. I will repay sayeth the Lord." The apostle continues (Romans 13:4): "The ruler . . . beareth not the sword in vain for he is . . . a revenger to execute wrath on him that doeth evil." (Elsewhere the Gospels favor turning the other cheek.) Paul clearly opposed individual revenge, but endorsed retribution by the ruler who "beareth not the sword in vain." Even if revenge motivated the retributive punishment of murderers, it would be irrelevant to the justice, or validity, of the punishment. Motives are irrelevant to the justice (deservedness) of what they motivate and retribution is independent of the motive of revenge. . . .

Religious objections to the death penalty reflect the Zeitgeist more than theology. In his Summa Theologica Thomas

Aquinas writes: "a man shall be sentenced to death for crimes of irreparable harm." In his Summa Contra Gentiles Thomas points out that "[murderers] may be justly executed. . . . [T]hey also have, at the critical point of death, the opportunity to be converted to God through repentance." (They did not give this opportunity to their victims.)

Trendy abolitionists often conflate two different virtues, justice and charity. They must be distinguished. Justice tries to mete out what is deserved. Charity impels us to love and help regardless of desert. Religion enjoins compassion and forgiveness, even of murderers, but does not suggest that justice should be replaced by compassion. Scripture presents God as legislator and judge who imparts *Justitia Misericordiae Dulcore Temperata:* Justice tempered by mercy, but not replaced by it.

Abolition of the death penalty would promise prospective murderers, that we will never do to them what they will do to their victims. Such a promise seems unwise as well as immoral.

"Intentional killing of humans is a radical no to personhood. It undercuts the ethical universe itself."

The Death Penalty Violates the Sanctity of Life

John Kavanaugh

In the following viewpoint, John Kavanaugh maintains that the death penalty undermines basic ethical tenets because it calls for the depersonalization of humans. As with other forms of deliberate killing, the author argues, capital punishment requires that certain persons be treated as dispensable objects. Yet all human life is sacred and not expendable, contends Kavanaugh; to condone any intentional killing is to declare ethics and morality worthless. Kavanaugh is a columnist for *America*, a Jesuit magazine.

As you read, consider the following questions:

1. In what ways have certain groups of people been denigrated and dehumanized, according to Kavanaugh?
2. What does Kavanaugh believe should be the "grounding principle for ethical issues of life and death?"
3. How does the author view the right to self-defense?

From John Kavanaugh, "Killing Persons, Killing Ethics." This article was originally published in *America*, July 19–26, 1997, and is reprinted with permission from America Press, Inc.

"There comes a point when a human being has forfeited all claims to being human. Who knows when? But that lump of flesh has ceased to be human and has become a cancer on the body of society and must be killed to help cure the whole."

Thus ran an argument in favor of capital punishment offered in a letter to the editor published in *The Saint Louis Post Dispatch* in June 1997. It is the classic move of depersonalization that eases a conscience preparing to kill.

Efforts at Depersonalization

From ancient days to our own, this has been done. Non-Greeks were once labeled "barbarians," non-Chinese were "foreign devils," Chinese were "gooks," Germans were "Huns," Jews were "sub-human" in the Nazi primers given to the Hitler Youth, criminals were "vermin," fetuses were "blobs of protoplasm," the comatose were "vegetables," Africans were "savages," Communists were "monsters," capitalists were "pigs," British were "thugs," the I.R.A. were "moral animals," blacks and women were "property," Amerinds were "brutes."

Of course, these were all humans, despite the efforts at depersonalization. But even the acknowledgement of the enemy's humanity does not stop the logic of death. For the next tactic is to propose that there are certain kinds of humans that may be killed. They may be powerless, sick, unborn, hostile, criminal or threatening. But they must go.

There is always a reason, always a desired purpose for every killing: to defend my life, my name, my property, my family, my heritage, my race, my nation, my religion. In each case, a moral "absolute" is invoked: but it is never the absolute value of human life. The value of a person is the one value that is expendable. There is, after all, one thread of logic that unites the mind of Timothy McVeigh, found guilty of the abominable Oklahoma City terror, with those who seek his death: the view that there are acceptable, even commanding reasons to kill.

This is the constant pattern of evil, whether we eliminate a person or exterminate a people. In every case there is a "higher" value that provides exception to "Thou shalt not kill." Killing in the name of a "higher value," however, is a subtle killing of ethics itself. For in killing persons, the foundation of moral experience is itself violated.

To *do* ethics, to *be* ethical, presumes a radical affirmation of personal dignity. In every moral choice is an implicit yes to personal existence. But intentional killing of humans is a radical no to personhood. It undercuts the ethical universe itself.

The Limit Situation in Ethics

Let me suggest a grounding principle for ethical issues of life and death. Affirmation of the intrinsic value of persons and personal moral dignity require that we never negate the personhood of ourselves or others, that we never treat any person as a mere thing or object. If personal life is expendable, ethics is expendable.

Since killing a person is the definitive act of turning a living human into a dead thing, since such killing is the irreversible negation of a personal life, any ethics that allows it will corrupt ethics—which rests upon personal dignity—from within.

Inviolability of human life is the limit situation in ethics. If we violate it, we violate the moral order and the claims it makes upon us.

Such a moral absolute is, admittedly, a demanding one. This may be why it has always been rejected throughout history when men and women have found it more realistic to declare others dispensable.

The main objection to a principle of non-killing has involved the threat of an unjust enemy, whether criminal or warrior. May I or my family or my nation do nothing if our own lives are at stake? Ought we not give the greatest penalty for the greatest crimes? If we do not, doesn't this degrade our own value?

On Self-Defense

I propose this: It is a positive moral good to defend oneself. Even more, we may do everything in our power to defend ourselves, *short of* violating the foundational principle itself by intending to kill the aggressor. Aggression provides no exception. What atrocity in history has *not* been perpetrated in

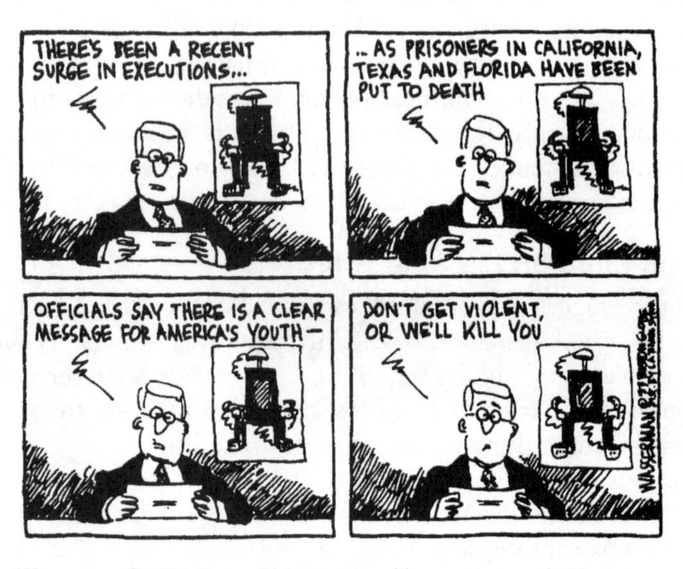

Wasserman. © 1998 *Boston Globe*. Reprinted by permission of Tribune Media Services.

the name of protection against real or imagined aggressors?

The deliberate will to kill a human is crucial here. The motive is murder, even if sincerely, courageously or self-righteously done. Although not all killings of humans are in every way equivalent, they do share one important thing: a reason to kill.

This absolute principle of non-killing is not a recommendation of passivity. Quite to the contrary, a primary commitment to the inherent dignity of personal life *drives* us to intervene on behalf of the defenseless or the victim. Our only moral limit is the direct intended killing of the aggressor.

It was much more the *lack* of commitment to intrinsic personal dignity that allowed people to stand by passively, not only when Hitler came to power, but also while he destroyed millions. It was Hitler who exploited the rationale of self-defense to justify his own outrages. And most of his followers swallowed his rationalizations of just punishments and just war. Such were the requirements of moral "realism."

Has there ever been a war that was not justified *by both*

sides? Has there ever been an assassination or act of terrorism that has not been rationalized by some logic of self-defense? Has there ever been a murder that has not had an excuse? My proposal is that it is always inexcusable.

Too unrealistic and heady, one might say. But a probe of the Gospels might yield a moral law more "unrealistic" and "unreasonable" yet.

VIEWPOINT

"The death penalty is a necessary tool that reaffirms the sanctity of human life while assuring that convicted killers will never again prey upon others."

The Death Penalty Affirms the Sanctity of Life

Michael D. Bradbury

In the following viewpoint, Michael D. Bradbury argues that criminals who commit heinous murders deserve a death sentence. Although many critics have recently claimed that arbitrary and unfair application of the death penalty warrants its abolition, capital punishment is actually quite even-handed, the author contends. Death sentences are subject to intensive reexaminations by both state and federal courts, and the decision to execute a criminal is never made lightly. Ultimately, however, it is the right of victims that are of primary importance in criminal justice decisions, maintains Bradbury. The death penalty affirms the value of human life by executing those who murder, he concludes. Bradbury is the district attorney of Ventura County, California.

As you read, consider the following questions:

1. As a district attorney, how does Bradbury arrive at a decision to seek the death penalty?
2. According to the author, how many innocent people have actually been executed?
3. In California, what kinds of resources do capital defendants have access to?

Reprinted, with permission, from Michael D. Bradbury, "The Death Penalty Is an Affirmation of the Sanctity of Life," *Los Angeles Times*, September 24, 2000.

"If we want to abolish the death penalty, let our friends the murderers take the first step."

Alphonse Karr,
19th century French novelist

A 2½-year-old girl was kidnapped, raped, sodomized, tortured and mutilated with vise grips over six hours. Then she was strangled to death. Her assailant, Theodore Frank, according to court records and his own admissions, had already molested more than 100 children during a 20-year period.

A sentence of death is the only appropriate punishment for such a serial assailant committing such an extraordinarily heinous crime. Two separate juries agreed, but now, more than 20 years after this horrendous murder, legal proceedings still continue in federal court.

Some Crimes Demand a Death Sentence

As district attorney of Ventura County (California) since 1978 and a prosecutor since 1967, I am convinced that there are some crimes that demand a sentence of death, despite recent publicity attacking the death penalty and calling for outright abolition or at least a "moratorium" until further studies are completed.

There have been 12 defendants sentenced to death in Ventura County while I have been district attorney. Their crimes included multiple murders and murders committed during the course of kidnappings and sexual assaults. These cases uniformly involve violent predators who attack the weakest, most defenseless members of our society. In one case, the defendant not only kidnapped and strangled the victim, but then committed a sex act on her dead body. In another case, an 8-year-old boy was kidnapped, sexually assaulted, strangled and then set on fire. In yet another horrific murder, an elderly husband and wife were bludgeoned in their own home during a robbery.

A decision to seek the death penalty is never made lightly. We thoroughly investigate both the crime and the defendant's background. I then make the final decision after considering the results of this exhaustive investigation and meeting with the assigned attorneys, investigators and other staff members. The defendant's attorneys are invited to appear at this meeting to present any information they consider relevant to the decision.

There will, of course, always be attacks on the death penalty. Some critics oppose it for moral or religious reasons, considerations that all persons have a right to decide for themselves. Other opponents claim "discriminatory enforcement"—that the death penalty is not imposed impartially among defendants of different races or backgrounds. More recently, capital punishment opponents have contended that seeking the death penalty means innocent people could be put to death. While I cannot claim to know every fact about the administration of the death penalty in other states, I would offer certain observations:

• There is a big difference between a case involving the exoneration of a defendant previously sentenced to death and one in which an innocent person is actually executed. The studies cited by death penalty opponents rely on cases where exoneration occurred before execution took place, not cases where any innocent people were actually executed. Thus, as one analyst commented, such studies appear to show that the most important error rate—innocent people who were actually executed—is zero.

Consider the Suffering of Victims

Charla's family raised her for 12 years—loved her, cared for her, watched her take her first baby steps, heard her laughter, saw the pictures she painted in school, dreamed of her future as she trembled on the brink of adolescence. All of this ended in 90 minutes of misery at the hands of a creature whose continued existence was an affront to humanity.

"They say executing [her killer] is so barbaric," shrugged Sherron King, mother of the murdered child. "Tell me what's barbaric. My daughter was alive (while being raped and choked). He won't even hear the sound of the bullets."

Don Feder, *Conservative Chronicle*, February 14, 1996.

• Death penalty opponents claim there are a great number of legal errors in death penalty trials. But all death verdicts are intensively reviewed by state and federal courts. The crucial issue is not whether such review ultimately discovers any technical error, but whether an alleged error in any way altered or prejudiced the ultimate jury verdict. That rarely occurs.

• Defendants charged with capital offenses in California receive high-quality representation. State law requires the provision of expert witnesses and investigator funds. Often, capital defendants retain leading experts in the scientific community to testify in their cases. Whenever a sentence of death is imposed, California law provides an automatic appeal to the state Supreme Court. At this stage, additional skilled and experienced attorneys are appointed to represent the defendant. If the state appeal is unsuccessful, another set of attorneys is appointed to take the case to federal court. These attorneys are given money for investigation and new experts.

• With the advent of DNA evidence, the chances of an innocent person being convicted and executed have been virtually eliminated in almost all cases where DNA evidence is available.

A Regard for Human Life

More than 130 years ago, the eminent philosopher John Stuart Mill spoke eloquently on this issue before the English Parliament: "Does fining a criminal show want of respect for property or imprisoning him, for personal freedom? Just as unreasonable is it to think that to take the life of a man who has taken that of another is to show want of regard for human life. We show, on the contrary, most emphatically our regard for it, by the adoption of a rule that he who violates that right in another forfeits it for himself."

In our understandable desire to be fair and to protect the rights of offenders in our criminal justice system, let us never ignore or minimize the rights of their victims. The death penalty is a necessary tool that reaffirms the sanctity of human life while assuring that convicted killers will never again prey upon others.

5

VIEWPOINT

"It is an act of unutterable cruelty to hold an individual in prison and to inform him that he will be put to death on a specified date."

The Death Penalty Is Cruel and Unusual Punishment

Peter L. Berger

The death penalty is cruel and inhumane, argues Peter L. Berger in the following viewpoint. Inmates awaiting execution experience mental torment; furthermore, capital punishment morally corrupts those who enforce and inflict it. Institutionalized execution is an act that no civilized society should tolerate, he concludes. Berger is director of the Institute for the Study of Economic Culture at Boston University and the author of *Redeeming Laughter: The Comic Dimension of Human Experience.*

As you read, consider the following questions:

1. In Berger's opinion, why should conservatives not be surprised by the suggestion that innocent people have been executed?
2. On what grounds should opposition to the death penalty be based, in the author's view?
3. In what way has the death penalty been "sanitized," according to Berger?

From Peter L. Berger, "Beyond the 'Humanly Tolerable,'" *National Review*, July 17, 2000;

For a long time, it has seemed that conservatives are as mindlessly enamored of the hangman as liberals are of the abortionist. Given recent developments, however, we may now see a break in at least the former affinity. It would be salutary if George W. Bush, the champion of "compassionate conservatism" and [as governor of Texas] the official in charge of the busiest assembly line of executions in the nation, were embarrassed by the sordid details that have come out of Texas. Perhaps he might even be induced to add a modest disclaimer to his bland assertion of confidence that no innocent person has ever been executed on his watch.

The evidence is rapidly mounting of the likelihood that innocent people have indeed been executed all along. And, as Carl M. Cannon said in the recent *National Review*, conservatives should not be surprised by this, since the judicial system, after all, is a branch of government: Conservatives have a supremely validated suspicion about government in all of its branches. It is almost an instinct of conservatives to distrust the wisdom of government, and therefore to limit its powers; surely this distrust should extend to this ultimate power over life and death.

A Conservative Principle

To limit the power of government to take life should be a conservative principle—and never mind if Jesse Jackson happens to agree with it. Cannon might have added that a large body of evidence suggests that the death penalty fails to deter, giving this particular exercise of governmental power a distinctively gratuitous character.

Opposition to the death penalty, in the United States as elsewhere, does in fact correlate with other liberal positions. One need have no sympathy with these other positions to agree on the death penalty, and one also need not agree with all the reasons given by liberals for their opposition. Clarence Darrow was an admirable character, but his famous defense of Leopold and Loeb was a masterpiece of mushy thinking: What he essentially said was that we are all animals determined by the laws of evolution—and therefore these two murderers should not be executed. [In the 1920s, Nathan Leopold and Richard Loeb were two affluent teens convicted of murdering a boy for the sport of it. They received life sentences instead of the death penalty.] The evolutionary maxim concerning the survival of the fittest in the struggle for existence seems to have escaped him (I would actually argue that Darrow was moved by compassion despite his rather silly philosophy). It is especially important to state that opposition to the death penalty is not necessarily linked to other "soft" attitudes toward crime (such as the notion that criminals are victims of society or that the judicial system should be a therapeutic institution). Opposition to the death penalty, I contend, should be based on much deeper grounds: on the perception that there are acts of cruelty that put in question our very humanity.

An Insidious Form of Torture

Executioner and condemned alike are dehumanized in today's executions. They are morally dead—dead as persons—even as their bodies move to the cadence of this modern dance macabre. Each participates in a peculiarly subtle and insidious form of torture that prepares them for their respective roles in the execution process. This is not justice but rather, in Albert Camus's wise reckoning, administrative murder. To be sure, these arrangements make executions easier and more palatable. Indeed, given our modern sensibilities, there may well be no other way we can execute a person. But at bottom these dehumanizing procedures hide a reality that we must face head on—namely, that the death penalty is utterly out of step with our current standards of decency and has no place in our justice system.

Robert Johnson, *Death Work*, 1998.

It is fair to assume that the overwhelming majority of Americans today are opposed to torture as a form of punishment. Why? It was, after all, a routine practice for much of history and, alas, is still routine in many countries today. One can imagine a social-scientific study showing that the prospect of torture would serve as an effective deterrent. One could also imagine certain judicial procedures to safeguard the innocent. I think (or, perhaps, as a pessimistic conservative, I should say that I hope) that the majority would still oppose torture, for the simple but crucial reason that this is a practice that offends our basic understanding of what is humanly tolerable. Of course, there are extreme cases that would put this understanding under pressure, as in the case of a captured terrorist who knows where an atomic bomb has been placed to go off. But here is another sound conservative principle—that good law must not be based on extreme cases.

An Act of Torture

And here is the critical insight relevant to this debate: The death penalty is an exercise of torture, superficially sanitized by the quasi-medical method of execution now prevalent in this country. It is an act of unutterable cruelty to hold an individual in prison and to inform him that he will be put to death on a specified date. To perceive the death penalty in this light is not the result of a philosophical or empirical argument. Rather, it is a primordial perception of the limits of what is humanly permissible. This perception, historically rooted in the Jewish and Christian view of the human condition, took a long time to mature and to be disseminated among significant numbers of people. An analogous case is the slow maturation of the perception that slavery is humanly intolerable. Slavery, torture, and the death penalty share this quality of an act that demeans those who inflict it as it degrades and torments those subjected to it. No civilized society should institutionalize such acts. In the matter of the death penalty, the United States today stands virtually alone among democracies, in the company of a repulsive collection of tyrannies. It is no wonder that American preachments about human rights are treated with derision by many, especially in Europe and Latin America, who share American democratic values. Perhaps—and I say so with minimal optimism—the current debate over the death penalty will lead to a situation that will allow Americans to find other areas in which to affirm their exceptionalism.

6

VIEWPOINT

"How is executing Karla Faye Tucker by lethal injection any [more] cruel than the way she used a pick-ax to viciously butcher two people to death?"

The Death Penalty Is Not Cruel and Unusual Punishment

Michael Scaljon

The death penalty is a constitutional and evenhanded form of punishment, contends Michael Scaljon in the following viewpoint. Rather than being "cruel and unusual," capital punishment actually treats murderers with more kindness and dignity than their victims receive. To stop executing those who have committed brutal crimes would put society at risk, the author concludes. At the time this viewpoint was written, Scaljon was a student majoring in government at the University of Texas in Austin.

As you read, consider the following questions:

1. According to Scaljon, what was the last year when more blacks than whites were executed?
2. What did the U.S. Supreme Court rule in *Furman vs. the State of Georgia*, according to the author?
3. What is *lex talionis*, according to Scaljon?

Reprinted, with permission, from Michael Scaljon, "Liberals, Death-Penalty Supporters Endanger Society," *Daily Texan*, July 2, 1998.

The state of Texas executes dozens of death row inmates each year. And every year many liberals question the morality of executing convicted felons for capital offenses. They argue that the death penalty is unjust and unconstitutional because it is a cruel and unusual punishment. These arguments and the points they raise are factually baseless.

Organizations dedicated to eliminating the death penalty have sprouted up around the country. In fact, there is even a student organization at the University of Texas called the Campaign to End the Death Penalty. Misguided and determined, they make exaggerated claims in pursuit of their unpopular campaign.

For example, Quent Reese, a member of this group, said in the February 10, 1998 edition of *The Daily Texan* that "a disproportionate number of poor people and minorities are executed."

But according to the 1996 edition of the *Sourcebook of Criminal Justice Statistics*, only 23 of the 56 inmates executed in 1995 were ethnic minorities. That is hardly a disproportionate number of minority executions. In fact, 1961 was the last year when more blacks were executed than whites.

The Death Penalty Is Constitutional

Contrary to what these critics imply, the death penalty is constitutional and used in a just manner. In the 1972 U.S. Supreme Court decision of *Furman vs. the State of Georgia*, the court declared that three options were available regarding the death penalty: a mandatory death sentence for certain crimes, development of standardized guidelines for juries, or outright abolition. Another case, *Gregg vs. the State of Georgia*, created guidelines for determining whether a convicted criminal should get the death penalty. The highest court in the land has ensured that the death penalty is evenhanded and fair—it is rather hard to argue with that.

In the same interview [mentioned above], Reese also claimed that the death penalty is "a way for the people at the top to scapegoat the problems of society—like poverty, homelessness and hunger—that give rise to crime."

No one has ever been executed in America for being poor, homeless or hungry; in fact, the last time a felon was executed for a crime other than murder was in 1964. No rapists, thieves or drug dealers have been executed since then. By using the death penalty, America is hardly scapegoating the problems of society—rather the courts are weeding out the absolute worst elements of society and punishing them accordingly.

A Humane Death

Nitrogen asphyxiation is . . . a perfect method of execution. It uses a cheap and universally available working medium that requires no special environmental precautions for its storage and disposal. Its first symptom is loss of conscious sensation, a primary goal in a humane execution. It involves no physical trauma, no toxic drugs; the executed man's organs will even be suitable for donation, a factor cited in a recent stay of execution for a Georgia killer.

Assuming that the prisoner's guilt has been sufficiently proved, nitrogen asphyxiation is perhaps the most gentle way to deal with him. A condemned man awaiting death by nitrogen asphyxiation would experience no more pain or suffering than he created in his own mind.

Stuart A. Creque, *National Review*, September 30, 1995.

The most common argument against the death penalty is that execution in any form is cruel and unusual punishment. The argument makes no sense at all. How is executing Karla Faye Tucker by lethal injection any [more] cruel than the way she used a pick-ax to viciously butcher two people to death? Liberals should be thankful that the death penalty isn't based on the Biblical premise of *lex talionis* (the punishment should fit the crime). Tucker, Steven Renfro and other recently executed criminals have died with more dignity and grace than they allowed their victims. With this system, criminals get off easy.

The simple fact is that the death penalty is an effective and just way to mete out punishment for heinous crimes. Those who commit brutal crimes should be put to death and not executing them puts all of society in danger.

VIEWPOINT

"Retribution means paying back, making restitution to a victim of what has been unjustly taken away."

Executions Deliver Reasonable Retribution

Pat Buchanan

The decision to execute a murderer is an act of just retribution, not revenge, argues Pat Buchanan in the following viewpoint. If the death penalty were truly vengeful, criminals would be executed by the same means that they used to kill their victims. Through capital punishment, the state impartially "pays back" what a murderer has wrongly taken away, Buchanan contends. Buchanan is a nationally syndicated columnist.

As you read, consider the following questions:

1. Why did Pat Robertson and Jerry Falwell urge mercy in the case of convicted murderer Karla Faye Tucker, according to Buchanan?
2. In the author's view, why is the arbitrary application of the death penalty irrelevant?
3. What would have become of Karla Faye Tucker had her death sentence been commuted, in Buchanan's opinion?

From Pat Buchanan, "Death Penalty Is Act of Retribution, Not Revenge," *Conservative Chronicle*, February 18, 1998. Reprinted by permission of Pat Buchanan and Creators Syndicate.

As the lethal injection raced toward the heart of Karla Faye Tucker, the husband of the woman Karla murdered exulted: "Here she comes, babydoll. She's all yours. The world's a better place."

Cold, hard, cruel, unforgiving, the words may be, but the hatred of Richard Thornton is understandable. For Karla Faye, the woman who killed his wife, had become famous and loved. Her impending execution had become a national melodrama, eliciting pleas for mercy all over the world. In death, she would be mourned by millions. Books would be written about her, movies made. And in them all, Karla Faye would emerge as the heroine.

Thornton's wife, Deborah, however, was not given 15 years to reconcile with her God. She was not even given 15 minutes as Karla Faye beat her to death with a pickax in 1983. Thus, undeniably, justice was done.

Mercy or Justice?

But the questions raised by the execution of this born again Christian who confessed to her crimes, cooperated with prosecutors, apologized for the evil she had done and spent her years on death row counseling other women are several: Should the claims of mercy have trumped the commands of justice? Was it better to execute Karla Faye than let her live out her days in prison doing the good she might have done? Was the 38-year-old woman Texas put to death in February 1998 really the same woman who mutilated Deborah Thornton in 1983?

Pat Robertson and Jerry Falwell urged mercy, while [then] Gov. George W. Bush refused to grant a 30-day reprieve to let the Texas Parole Board review its 16-0 decision to let the execution proceed.

Opponents of capital punishment have used the intercession of Christians on Karla's behalf to accuse them of selective indignation. You cry for mercy for this pretty woman of your own faith, they say, but never for the poor, friendless, black male facing execution.

But the charge is unfair, the point irrelevant. All of us take a greater interest in what happens to those close to us, be it a family member, friend or member of one's community, than with what happens to someone we do not know or with whom we are unable easily to identify. That is human and natural.

Karla Faye Tucker attracted national attention because the hideousness of her crime contrasted so with her new persona and because she was articulate, mediagenic and feminine. In Western society, there has always been a revulsion at using violence against women, which is why we do not permit them in combat and why the rescue of "women and children first" is an unwritten commandment.

Not a Form of Revenge

Opponents of capital punishment tend to describe it as a surrender to our emotions—to grief, rage, fear, blood lust. For most supporters of the death penalty, this is exactly false. Even when we resolve in principle to go ahead, we have to steel ourselves. Many of us would find it hard to kill a dog, much less a man. Endorsing capital punishment means not that we yield to our emotions but that we overcome them. (Immanuel Kant, the great advocate of the death penalty precisely on moral grounds, makes this point in his reply to the anticapital-punishment reformer Cesare Beccaria—accusing Beccaria of being "moved by sympathetic sentimentality and an affectation of humanitarianism.") If we favor executing murderers it is not because we want to but because, however much we do not want to, we consider ourselves obliged to.

David Gelernter, *Commentary*, April 1998.

That imposition of the death penalty is arbitrary is also true but equally irrelevant. Since it was reinstated in 1976, there have been 400,000 murders in America but only 436 executions. Capital punishment may be more common in Texas and Florida than in other states. But that only tells us states have different traditions and laws. It would be preposterous for a serial killer like Ted Bundy to argue that had he perpetrated his atrocities in New York, he might have escaped death and therefore his sentence was cruel.

If there is any bias in imposing the death penalty, it is a bias against males. Of those 436 executed, only one was a woman. If there is hypocrisy here, it is the hypocrisy of feminists. Why aren't they demanding fairer representation on death row?

An Act of Retribution

As Karla Faye neared death, we heard the old refrain that this would be "legalized murder," an act of "revenge" that no decent and humane society should tolerate. Such commentary shows a loss of moral coherence. The death penalty for Karla Faye Tucker was no more legalized murder than her imprisonment was legalized kidnapping. Nor was her death an act of revenge. It was an act of retribution, and the distinction between retribution and revenge is as great as that between civilization and barbarism.

In Karla Faye's case, revenge would have been the ax murder of her, or her husband, by Richard Thornton. Retribution means paying back, making restitution to a victim of what has been unjustly taken away. As we cannot restore the life of Deborah Thornton, the one who brutally took that life, Karla Faye Tucker, makes restitution by giving up her own. Retribution is imposed, not by the Thornton family but by an impartial state acting in the name of society.

Would society have been better served by the commutation of Karla Faye Tucker's sentence? As the palpable anguish of Gov. Bush showed, it was not an easy question. But had her sentence been commuted in an act of mercy, Karla Faye, ax-murderess, would have lived a life of celebrity and surely, one day not too far distant, would have been released by popular demand. Would that have been justice?

8

VIEWPOINT

"We do not . . . stab, shoot, throw acid, maim, or mug persons convicted of such aggravated assaults. Where, then, is the rational logic for retention of the death penalty?"

Executions Do Not Deliver Reasonable Retribution

Marvin E. Wolfgang

The death penalty does not provide a rational form of retribution for the crime of murder, Marvin E. Wolfgang contends in the following viewpoint. For one thing, true retribution would be restorative, but a murder victim's life is not restored by executing the murderer. Moreover, Wolfgang argues, criminal justice does not require the offender to suffer the exact effects of the crime he committed—rapists are not punished by being raped, for example. Instead, criminals are generally punished by being deprived of liberty, and the length of their deprivation corresponds to the severity of their crime. Capital punishment, therefore, is out of step with the logic of criminal justice system, the author maintains. Wolfgang is a professor of law and criminology at the University of Pennsylvania.

As you read, consider the following questions:

1. What is *lex talionis*, according to Wolfgang?
2. According to the author, what is the principle of proportional sentencing?
3. How does the state actually undermine the effects of punishment by executing murderers, in Wolfgang's opinion?

Excerpted from Marvin E. Wolfgang, "We Do Not Deserve to Kill," *Crime and Delinquency*, January 1998.

There is no rationale of punishment or disposition of a convicted offender that requires the death penalty. No logic of any rationale leads ineluctably to the death penalty. What are these rationales? Retribution, expiation, the utilitarian notion of deterrence, rehabilitation, social protection, or defense. We know they are not mutually exclusive except in abstract analysis, perhaps not even in that.

Several of these I should like to dispense with quickly because either the argument of the rationale clearly does not lead to the death penalty, or the evidence required to support the argument for the death penalty is weak, inadequate, or inconclusive. Death is not expiatory for the offender, for expiation implies that the offender has atoned for his guilt and is now cleansed in this life so he is free to accept the grace of God or a God-surrogate in the name of the state. Rehabilitation also requires life to continue so the former offending person can be restored to a life of social conformity. Deterrence is an unproven case. The Committee on Deterrent and Incapacitative Effects, of the National Research Council, National Academy of Science, concluded, after extensive research on crime in general and the death penalty in particular, that "in summary, the flaws . . . lead the Panel to conclude that the results of the analyses on capital punishment provide no useful evidence on the deterrent effect of capital punishment."

What is left? Social protection and retribution. But social protection is so closely linked to deterrence and the utilitarian position that we need not pursue it further. Moreover, the social protection argument can lead to the undesirable consequences of executing potentially "dangerous" violent offenders and those who, as in the case of the Soviet penal code of the late 1920s and early 1930s, are "socially dangerous" to the state, even though they may not have committed any other specifically designated capital crime.

Retribution Theory

Retribution would appear to contain the most reasonable logic leading to the death penalty. Part of the reasoning in retribution theory includes [English philosopher Thomas] Hobbes's notion of establishing an equilibrium, of restoring the state of being to what it had been before the offensive behavior had been committed. Strict homeostasis cannot be achieved with the death penalty for, as we all know, the victim of a killing cannot be restored. Nor is the abstract sense of equilibrium satisfied by execution, that is, the *lex talionis*, eye for an eye, tooth for a tooth. For retribution requires pain equal to that inflicted on the victim, plus an additional pain for committing the crime, crossing the threshold from law-abiding to law-violative behavior.

Execution Does Not Resolve Loss

We must ask ourselves, Does killing the criminal honor the victim? Does it enhance the lives of a victim's family? Is it a constructive or appropriate method of dealing with anger? No. I recall one woman who, regarding the criminal convicted of killing one of her family members, said, "I don't believe that killing him is going to make my loss any less." In that statement this insightful woman acknowledges the reality that executing the criminal will not bring back a loved one nor will it take away the pain.

Renato Martino, *Origins*, March 18, 1999.

The state's killing of a convicted offender, especially under the medically protective circumstances now used, is not likely to cause him as much pain as he inflicted on his victim. Even if the pain to each were the same, the second requirement of retribution is not met—namely, the pain to be inflicted for the crime per se. What then would meet the requirement? A torturous execution? Perhaps, but that solution conflicts with other attitudes in our society, particularly those concerned with physical assaults by or in the name of the state. Apparently, Western society considers corporal punishment an anathema of civilization. We permit the police to shoot at fleeing felons under certain circumstances, but even this act is discouraged unless life is endangered. Physical force may be used to arrest a suspect. But once a suspect is arrested, we mount glorious attacks against any physical abuse of arrestees, detainees, and defendants. We decry inadequate diets and urge good medical care for prisoners. The philosophy of our health delivery system is such that we must present our sacrifice to the rationalization for death in good physical condition. The state has made efforts to reduce the suffering of death in most exquisite ways.

Thus, there is a strong cultural opposition to corporal punishment. Western society today would not tolerate, I am sure, cutting off limbs, gouging out eyes, or splitting the tongue. Even for murder, there would be opposition to "partial execution" (i.e., cutting off legs, cutting of the penis, etc.). If we cringe at the thought of eliminating part of the corporal substance, is it logical to eliminate the total corpus?

Proportional Sentencing

A principal part of the rationale of retribution is proportional sentencing. Cesare Beccaria, Jeremy Bentham, and other rationalists recognized the principle. The "just desserts" or "commensurate desserts" model amply anticipates it. Beccaria's scales of seriousness of crime and severity of sanction were meant to be proportional. Equal punishment for equal crime does not mean that the punishment should be exactly like the crime but that the ratios of sanction severity should have a corresponding set of ratios of crime seriousness.

Moreover, punishment can or should be expressed in equivalences rather than in the same physical form of the crime. For example, we do not prescribe state-inflicted injuries for offenders who have injured but not killed their victims. It is not banal to argue this point because it is critical to the logic of capital punishment. If the victim has been assaulted and then treated by a physician and discharged or is hospitalized, the state does not exact the same penalty for the offender. We do not in the name of the state stab, shoot, throw acid, maim, or mug persons convicted of such aggravated assaults. Where, then, is the rational logic for retention of the death penalty for inflicting death?

Instead, equivalences in pain are sought in kind, not in physical exactitude. The common commodity of pain in our democratic society is deprivation of liberty over time, measured in days, months, and years. Other forms of deprivation are subsumed under this deprivation. It is but a reasonable extension of the equivalences between deprivation of liberty for crimes less than murder and the same deprivation for longer periods of time for the crime of homicide.

In the Beccarian mode, more can be said about the "pains of imprisonment." Death eliminates all. It does away with guilt, frustration, aspiration achievement disparities, desires for unattained and unattainable things, anxieties, and fears. By execution, the state deprives itself of the functioning of these self-inflicted punishments and of those punishments derived from the deprivation of liberty. Death ends all pain, and the offender is punished no more.

Periodical Bibliography

The following articles have been selected to supplement the diverse views presented in this chapter. Addresses are provided for periodicals not indexed in the *Readers' Guide to Periodical Literature*, the *Alternative Press Index*, the *Social Sciences Index*, or the *Index to Legal Periodicals and Books*.

Jonathan Alter	"The Death Penalty on Trial," *Newsweek*, June 12, 2000.
Robert E. Burns	"Pull the Plug on the Death Penalty," *U.S. Catholic*, August 1998.
Ann Coulter	"Resort to Familiar Innocence Pleadings," *Washington Times*, July 2, 2000.
Carol Fennelly	"To Die For," *Sojourners*, July/August 1998.
Eric M. Freedman	"The Case Against the Death Penalty," *USA Today*, March 1, 1997.
David Gelernter	"What Do Murderers Deserve?" *Commentary*, April 1998.
David Gergen	"Death By Incompetence," *U.S. News and World Report*, June 26, 2000.
Issues and Controversies on File	"Update: Death Penalty," September 15, 2000.
Ed Koch	"Capital Punishment for Capital Crime," *Newsday*, January 13, 2000.
David Leibowitz	"Death Penalty Showdown: It Is Just, Legal, and Supported by a Majority," *Arizona Republic*, May 16, 1999.
Joshua Micah Marshall	"Death in Venice," *The New Republic*, July 31, 2000.
John O'Sullivan	"A Logical and Just Practice," *National Review*, July 17, 2000.
Felix G. Rohatyn	"America's Deadly Image," *Washington Post*, February 20, 2001.
Eric Ruder	"Death Penalty on Trial," *International Socialist Review*, Spring 2000.

CHAPTER 3

Is the Death Penalty an Effective Deterrent?

Chapter Preface

During the 2000 presidential campaign, Republican candidate George W. Bush and Democratic candidate Al Gore each expressed strong support for the death penalty. In the third presidential debate, when asked why they backed the death penalty, both candidates answered: "It's a deterrence." Without capital punishment, they maintain, murders would increase.

Many U.S. political leaders agree with Bush and Gore. For example, when Republican George E. Pataki became governor of New York in 1995, he reinstated the death penalty there, arguing that "for too long, [murderers] were not subject to swift and certain punishment and, as a result, violent criminal acts were not deterred." Within just one year, Pataki points out, the restored death penalty led to a dramatic drop in violent crime: assaults went down 22 percent, and murders dropped by nearly one-third. Statistics from other states lend support to Pataki's claims. In Texas in 1980, just before executions were resumed, the murder rate was eighteen per 100,000 people. After nearly twenty years, the rate dropped to nine per 100,000. The city of Houston, Texas, had 701 murders in 1980; by 1998, the number of murders had dropped to 241.

Death penalty critics dispute these statistics, however. Many contend that other factors, such as an increase in the rate of convictions and stepped-up crime-control measures, account for the drop in murder rates. A 1996 survey of seventy leading American criminologists found that more than 80 percent of them claimed the death penalty does not lower homicide rates. Moreover, a *New York Times* survey completed in the year 2000 revealed that the twelve states without the death penalty have murder rates that are below the national average. As anti-death-penalty activist Richard Dieter explains, "the average murder rate . . . in 1998 among states with the death penalty was 6.2 per 100,000. However, the average murder rate among states without the death penalty was only 3.2 per 100,000. A look at neighboring death-penalty and non-death-penalty states shows similar trends."

Criminologists and politicians continue to have strong disagreements about the alleged deterrent effect of the death penalty, and both proponents and critics of capital punishment seem to have powerful evidence to support their conclusions. The following chapter takes a closer look at this compelling and conflicting information.

1

VIEWPOINT

"The obvious conclusion from looking at the statistics . . . is that capital punishment does *deter murder."*

The Death Penalty Deters Crime

Jay Johansen

Statistics reveal that the death penalty deters crime, argues web developer Jay Johansen in the following viewpoint. Between 1965 and 1982, when there were very few executions in the United States, the homicide rate steadily increased. When the number of executions sharply increased in 1983 and 1996, the homicide rate fell. Such consistent correlation between homicide rates and executions is not a result of coincidence—it is proof that capital punishment works, the author asserts.

As you read, consider the following questions:

1. When did the U.S. Supreme Court reinstate capital punishment?
2. In what year did the homicide rate have its biggest one-year drop, according to Johansen?
3. In his discussion of relevant data, why does the author cite the homicide rate rather than just the simple number of homicides?

Reprinted, with permission, from Jay Johansen, "Does Capital Punishment Deter Crime?" March 29, 1998, web article found at http://my.voyager.net/jayjo/capdeter.htm.

Advocates of capital punishment routinely argue that statistics prove that it deters crime. Opponents of capital punishment just as routinely argue that statistics prove that it does not.

I suppose a naive person might find this disagreement puzzling. Even if we cannot agree on moral questions, surely we could at least agree on basic facts. I mean, it would be understandable if an anti-capital punishment person said that, yes, it does deter crime, but it is still wrong because it is cruel and barbaric; or if a pro-capital punishment person said, okay, it doesn't deter crime any more than life imprisonment or some other punishment, but it is still right because it is just. But can't we at least agree on the underlying facts?

But as I'm sure we're all aware these days, you can twist statistics to prove almost anything. Statisticians have developed many sophisticated techniques to carefully analyze data. People with a point to prove can abuse these techniques to distort the data.

But I'm a simple guy, so I decided to look at the simple statistics. Let's just look at the raw numbers: no clever analysis, no involved mathematical manipulation, just look at the numbers.

So, using statistics from the United States Department of Justice website, here's my graph number 1: The homicide rate for each year since 1950. The rate is given as the number of homicides for every million people.

A casual glance at this graph clearly shows that homicide rates increased sharply beginning about 1965 or 1966, they took a steep dive from 1980 to 1985, started back up again until 1991–1992, and now appear to be inching down.

Surely a reasonable, concerned person could ask if there is any apparent cause for the sudden sharp increase in the late 60's. And surely we could look with hope at the drop in the early 80's, and ask if there was not something that was happening then that we could reproduce.

So let's look at another graph. Graph number 2 shows the homicide rate, just as above, and on top of this I show the number of cases where capital punishment was imposed.

Note the interesting correlations. The number of executions plummeted from 47 in 1962 to 2 in 1967 to zero in

Graph 1: Homicide Rate

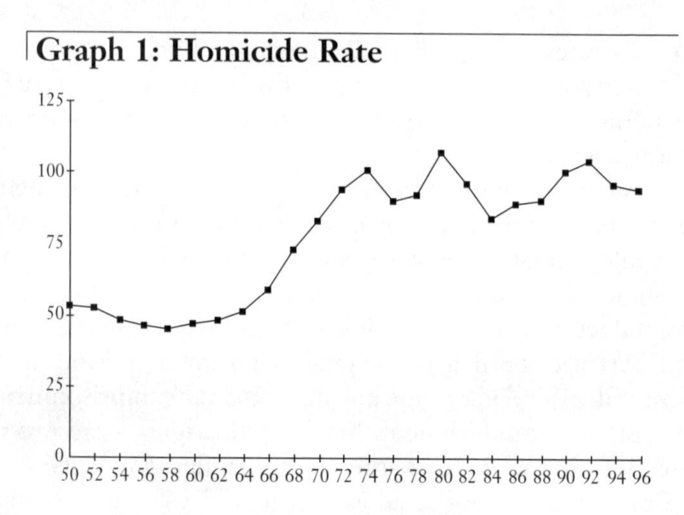

United States Department of Justice, Bureau of Justice Statistics, 1998.

1968. The homicide rate, which had been holding steady around 5 throughout the 50's, started up in 1965, just two years after executions began their plummet. The biggest increase in one year came in 1967, the same year that the last person was executed.

So okay, maybe this was simply a coincidence. Capital punishment was reinstated a decade later. What happened then?

In 1976 the Supreme Court issued several decisions in

Graph 2: Homicide Rate vs. Executions

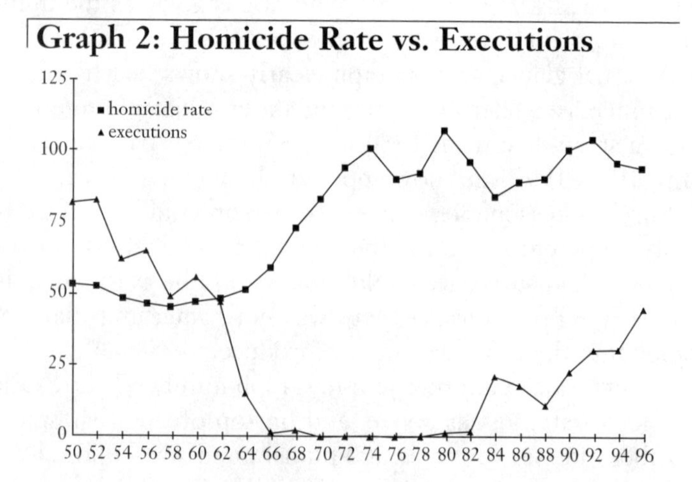

United States Department of Justice, Bureau of Justice Statistics, 1998.

which they basically backtracked and again allowed capital punishment. (They didn't quite say that they were changing their minds or admitting error, but rather that the flaws which they had discovered in the previous capital punishment laws had now been corrected.) The first person was actually executed in 1977. In the very year of these Supreme Court decisions, the homicide rate plummeted. But no more than two people were actually executed in any one year through 1982, and so perhaps criminals concluded that the danger of execution was remote, and the homicide rate crawled back up. Then the number of executions suddenly went up in 1983, and in that year the homicide rate showed its biggest one-year drop. With the sudden surge in executions in 1996, the homicide rate again fell.

More than Just Coincidence

Indeed, just looking at this graph we can see that the homicide rate is almost the mirror image of the number of executions. Consistently when the number of executions goes down, the homicide rate goes up, and when the number of executions goes up, the homicide rate goes down. The only major exception to this is the fall in homicides in 1976, which came *before* executions re-started. But this is easily explainable by the fact that the court decisions allowing executions to resume came a year or two before executions actually did resume. Criminals may have been responding to press reports that capital punishment was once again going to take place, in advance of it actually happening.

I'm sure that opponents of capital punishment will say that my analysis here is too simplistic; that I have failed to take other factors into account; that this correlation between execution rates and homicide rates is pure coincidence, and that other factors explain why homicide rates went up and down at these times that had nothing to do with the number of executions.

To which I reply, Well, maybe, but I think you have an awfully hard sell. If there was just one point of correlation, it might be explained by coincidence. That is, if the homicide rate had gone up when capital punishment was abolished, but when capital punishment was re-instated the homicide rate had remained unchanged, or had gone up further, one might reasonably say that the first correlation was simply coincidence. But when we can clearly see that the two numbers mirror each other, consistently over a period of almost fifty years, attributing this to coincidence gets pretty hard to believe.

The obvious conclusion from looking at the statistics, without any fancy "analysis" or "factoring out of other factors," is that capital punishment *does* deter murder.

Selection of Data

Lest I be accused of the same offense of which I accuse others, I will here freely discuss how I selected the data which I present.

I used homicide rate, i.e., homicides per million people, rather than the simple number of homicides, for two reasons. One, the data from the Department of Justice presented the numbers that way, so it was easiest to just take their numbers as given rather than looking up the population of the country each year and computing the simple number. (And I also would have run into the problem of possibly using different population statistics than the Department of Justice did, and thus introducing errors into the data.) Second, this is a good way to present the data anyway as it reflects the likelihood that any one person will decide to commit murder, which is the question under consideration. A graph of the simple number of murders would presumably show an overall upward trend reflecting growing population, and thus masking any deterrence or lack of deterrence.

On the other hand I used the simple number of executions rather than any "execution rate." Arguably it would be more accurate to plot executions as a percentage of the number of homicides, to show the probability that any given murderer would, in fact, be executed. I didn't do this for the simple reason that the Department of Justice figures did not present the numbers this way, and to compute them I would have had to convert homicide rate to number of homicides, and then compare this number to number of executions. This would have involved a lot of calculation using statistics from other sources, and so would not only have been a lot of work but could have introduced errors as mentioned above.

I converted homicide rates from homicides per 100,000, as the Department of Justice tabulates them, to homicides per million, simply to allow me to plot both homicide rates and number of executions on the same scale. That is, this conversion put the homicide rates in the 50 to 100 range or so, and executions were in the 0 to 100 range, so this conversion made it possible to plot both on the same graph without one being reduced to a line barely distinguishable from zero.

Time Range

A more serious criticism could be leveled at my selection of the time range to include. I could not find any data on executions before 1930 or after 1996, so that was the widest possible range I could use. Clearly I had to go before the mid-60's to get before-and-after abolition comparisons, so going back to 1950 seemed about the shortest range to give meaningful numbers for comparison, and I went through the latest numbers because we surely want to see where things are right now.

Lest you wonder, analysis of earlier numbers reveals that the homicide rate went up sharply in the 20's and early 30's and fell in the late 30's and 40's. As I don't have data on executions before 1930, I cannot say if there is any correlation between the execution rate then and this increase. There were increasing numbers of executions in the late 30's as the homicide rate was coming down, but the correlation is nowhere near as obvious or dramatic as it is for the time period I discuss in the body of this viewpoint. Thus, I conclude that the movement of homicide rates in the 30's probably cannot be entirely explained by any deterrent effect of capital punishment, but must be at least partly attributed to other factors. I do not see this as in any way a refutation of the point of this viewpoint: neither I nor any one else I have ever heard is claiming that the deterrent effect of capital punishment is the *only* thing which affects homicide rates, merely that it is an important factor. No one denies that there could be other factors.

If anyone wants to accuse me of "cooking the data" to bias the results, based on the above or other considerations, that is your privilege. But I think in fairness you must show some equally simple, defensible selection of data that shows *no* correlation between capital punishment and murder rates. Otherwise, I think you can fairly be accused of saying simply, "That data *must* be invalid because it does not agree with what I just *know* must be true. No further analysis is necessary."

2

VIEWPOINT

"The death penalty has absolutely nothing to do with crime rates."

The Death Penalty Does Not Deter Crime

Part I: Christine Notis; Part II: Edward Hunter

The authors of the following two-part viewpoint assert that the death penalty does not deter violent crime. In Part I, Iowa State University biology student Christine Notis argues that because only a fraction of death-row prisoners are actually executed, murderers do not feel hindered by the threat of capital punishment. Moreover, she points out, homicide rates are actually higher in those states that enforce the death penalty. In Part II, freelance journalist Edward Hunter cites a study concluding that capital punishment is no more effective than life imprisonment as a crime deterrent. This article was written as a news release from the University of Florida. The opinions expressed by Dr. Radelet do not necessarily reflect the opinion of the author or the university.

As you read, consider the following questions:

1. According to Notis, how many of the 3,054 prisoners sentenced to death in 1995 were executed?
2. Which three states have the highest murder rate in the United States, according to Notis?
3. According to Michael Radelet, quoted by Hunter, how much does it cost to execute a prisoner in Florida?

Part I: Reprinted, with permission, from Christine Notis, "Is the Death Penalty an Effective Deterrent?" 1997 web article found at www.public.iastate.edu/~cnotis/penalty.htm. Endnotes and references in the original have been omitted in this reprint. *Part II:* Reprinted, with permission, from Edward Hunter, "Experts Agree: Death Penalty Not a Deterrent to Violent Crime," January 15, 1997, web article found at www.napa.ufl.edu/oldnews/death1.htm.

I

The issue of the death penalty is a hot debate around the country. Arguments against the death penalty include the following: (1) it is morally wrong to take anyone's life, (2) it does not deter crime, (3) it is racially and economically biased, and (4) it costs too much. In contrast, arguments for the death penalty are that (1) it is not morally wrong to kill those who have killed others, and (2) it does deter crime and it is not racially or economically biased. Some proponents of the death penalty do agree that the death penalty is not cost efficient at this time. However, they believe that the high costs can be overcome with the elimination of appeals. The morality question is a matter of opinion or religious beliefs. In contrast, the question of deterrence can be answered objectively using common sense and statistics. By analyzing different arguments for and against the death penalty, such as the "fear of death" myth, the cost of the death penalty, and the racial and economic bias of the death penalty, it can be shown that the death penalty is not an effective deterrent of crime.

The Deterrence Argument

According to S. Nathanson, the deterrence argument states that "although executing the murderer neither prevents the death of the victim nor restores their life, instating the death penalty effectively prevents the deaths of other victims." On the surface, this seems like a convincing argument, because of course, if the murderer is dead, then he/she will not kill again. The question is, though, does the death penalty prevent the potential killer from ever killing in the first place? Is it more effective than other forms of punishment? Supporters of the death penalty argue that the death penalty ensures that the murderer will not strike again. But doesn't life in prison without parole do the same? Proponents of the deterrence argument say that the death penalty prevents murders because the killers, like everyone else, have a fear of death. I do not believe that this is a valid statement. Everyone does things that are risks to his/her life. Driving a car, riding a bike, rock climbing, swimming, smoking—we do these things for the need to get places, for adventure, excitement, pleasure, or out of mere habit, even though we know that they place some risk on our lives. It is also true, then, that murderers place risks on their lives when they kill. But just like everybody else, they do not stop what they are doing because there is a risk of death.

If the death penalty was administered more often, or if it was given to everyone who committed murder, then it would be a different story. If you knew that if you killed someone, you would automatically be executed, you might choose not to kill. The fact is, though, that it is not certain that all murderers will be executed. Some will be found innocent, some sentences will be appealed, and some defendants will be found insane, and not even go to jail. The point is that right now murderers are not faced with the certainty of their deaths, but with only a risk. This is just like driving a car or smoking. In 1995, a total of 3,054 prisoners were sentenced to death. Of these individuals, only 56 were actually executed. It is hard to fear for your death when there is a very small risk of actually dying.

It is also worth noting that some murders are committed by those who do not rationally think about the consequences. These murders occur in the heat of passion, in a state of panic or drug use, or are committed by a mentally ill person. Under these circumstances, the murderer is most likely not thinking about the chance of dying as a result of their killing.

Which States Have Higher Murder Rates?

There have been a number of studies on whether states that have the death penalty actually have lower murder rates than states that don't have it. For example, from the years 1920 to 1958, Thorstein Sellin did a comparative study between states with and without the death penalty. In order to be as scientific as possible, Sellin compared states which were geographic neighbors and had similar economic and social aspects. Sellin concluded that there were no significant differences in homicide rates in the states with the death penalty and those without the death penalty.

Modern comparisons show that murder rates are higher in death penalty states than in non-death penalty states. The average murder rate per 100,000 people in 1994 among death penalty states was 8.0, and the average murder rate among non-death penalty states was only 4.4. Right now, the states that use the death penalty most often (Texas, Florida, and Georgia), have the highest murder rates in the country. If the death penalty actually deterred murders, we would expect to see opposite results.

The Death Penalty Is Expensive

If the death penalty was an effective deterrent, it would also be more cost efficient than any other forms of punishment. The fact is that a single execution costs more than two million dollars. This is $800,000 more than incarcerating a person for life. Supporters of the death penalty argue that the reason it is so expensive to execute someone is because of the numerous frivolous appeals. Proponents say that if the death penalty was applied properly, without so many appeals, it would be less expensive than life in prison without parole.

The truth is that these costs are not the result of frivolous appeals, but instead the result of necessary, Constitutionally mandated safeguards. In order to ensure a just conviction, (1) juries must be given clear guidelines on sentencing, (2) defendants have to have two trials, one to decide their guilt or innocence, the other, if proven guilty, to decide whether or not they should be sentenced to death, and (3) defendants that are sentenced to death are granted oversight protection in an automatic appeal to the Supreme Court. These safeguards result in a more drawn out jury selection process, an increase in the number of motions filed, more investigators and expert testimony, and more lawyers with specialization in death penalty cases. All of this taken together means that the trial will be a lot longer, thus, more expensive.

The economic impact has to be felt by someone, and it is usually not the defendant. It is the counties that usually pay for the prosecution, and because most defendants lack the needed funds, the counties usually pay for the defense as well. Because of these bills, some counties have to cut back on basic services, ironically including police protection, in order to pay for one capital murder trial.

In other words, the death penalty is not more cost effective than life in prison without parole. It seems to be almost hypocritical of our society to keep spending so much money on the death penalty. Isn't this the same society which strongly argues slight raises in taxes for good causes, like education and/or health care? Yet the tax payers in the United States continue to fork out their dough to see people fried or hanged.

The cost of the death penalty can be measured in more than just dollars and cents. Capital cases take up tremendous amounts of court time, thereby delaying the processing of other important cases. There is also a significant burden on the United States Supreme Court. Furthermore, State Supreme Court officials probably spend at least one-half of their time dealing with death penalty appeals.

Racial and Economic Bias

In addition to not being cost effective, the death penalty certainly does not give equal justice under the law. For it to be an effective deterrent, the death penalty must not be racially or economically biased. However, in a study by Joel Ricci in 1988, it was shown that "if you were a black man convicted of murdering a white man, you were four times as likely to receive the death penalty as a white man convicted of murdering a black." In May of 1994, the *New York Times* stated, "A report to Congress in March found that of the 37 people whom the Justice Department had sought to execute for drug-related murders since 1988, 33 of the 37 were black or Hispanic inmates, while three-fourths of those charged under this statute were white." As far as the total number of executions since 1976, 40% have been black, while 56% have been white. This may seem to reject the argument that the death penalty is racially biased, but keep in mind that blacks only constitute 11% of the United States's population. Thus, their execution rate is a lot higher than that of whites.

There are obviously signs of racism in the administration of the death penalty. It's very sad to see that this racism is still rooted in our society after all that has been done to get rid of it. Not only is this racism just plain wrong, but is also a contradiction of the equal rights amendment to the Constitution.

The issue of class, or economic status, is also a problem in death penalty cases. Defendants who have adequate funds are more likely to hire better, more experienced (and more expensive) lawyers than those defendants who do not have these funds. In February of 1991, the *New York Times* reported, "Most indigent defendants in capital cases are represented by inexperienced, ill-paid lawyers who do lackluster, routine work." Having an inexperienced lawyer increases the probability that the defendant will be sentenced to death. Therefore, it is possible to see how someone's economic status determines whether they will live or die.

The Death Penalty and Homicide Rates

States with the death penalty have higher murder rates than non-death-penalty states. Moreover, these rates have risen and fallen in similar patterns over the years, suggesting that capital punishment has little or no deterrent effect.

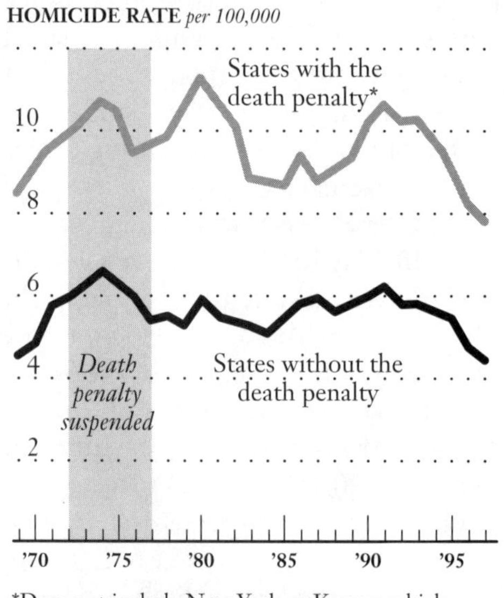

New York Times and National Center for Health Statistics and Census Bureau, 2000.

By evaluating the "fear of death" myth, the cost of the death penalty, and the racial and economic biases of the death penalty, we can see that it is likely not an effective deterrent of crime. If the death penalty is not an effective deterrent, then what is? If we use life sentences instead of the death penalty, we would all have a little extra money in our pockets, and we would be eliminating some racist and classist actions.

II

January 17, 1997 is the 20th anniversary of the first execution in the United States since the death penalty's reinstatement, and a University of Florida (UF) researcher's study shows 90 percent of the nation's top criminologists say killing people to deter violent crime is an immense waste of time and money.

"Among the experts, there is overwhelming consensus that the death penalty never has been, is not and never could be a deterrent to homicide over and above long imprisonment," said Michael Radelet, chairman of UF's sociology department and a longtime researcher of death penalty issues. "The rates of consensus were much higher on this question than I ever thought possible. We never see 90 percent of criminologists agree on anything."

It was on Jan. 17, 1977, that Gary Gilmore faced a Utah firing squad to become the first man executed in the United States since the Supreme Court again legalized the death penalty in 1976. From 1977 through Dec. 31, 1996, 357 other prisoners have been executed.

For the study, Radelet and UF sociology Professor Ronald Akers surveyed 67 current and former presidents of the top three criminology professional organizations—the American Society of Criminology, the Academy of Criminal Justice Sciences and the Law and Society Association. The study is published in the February 1997 *Journal of Criminal Law and Criminology*.

"We wanted to gauge the opinions of the people who know the literature and how the death penalty has been researched," Radelet said.

What Makes an Effective Deterrent?

He said people need to keep in mind what it means to have an effective deterrent—the penalty persuades a person not to commit a violent criminal act—and distinguish that from a retributive effect, or punishment for the criminal.

"Deterrence means that we execute people to send a message to others," Radelet said. "After a while, increases in the severity of punishment have decreasing incremental deterrent effect. So if you haven't deterred somebody by life, you're not going to deter them by death.

"If you want to deter people from leaning on your stove, medium heat works just as well as high heat."

Radelet said a large segment of the pro-death penalty community and numerous politicians regularly—and incorrectly—cite the death penalty's supposed deterrent effects in their arguments for continued executions.

"Politicians who say we need the death penalty to cut the crime rate or arguments of that sort are simply wrong," Radelet said. "The death penalty has absolutely nothing to do with crime rates. If politicians are serious about reducing high rates of criminal violence, they're barking up the wrong tree."

So why do people support the death penalty so fervently?

In addition to the retributive argument, Radelet says many death penalty supporters feel that without executions, the offender will be released from prison after serving a short sentence. When people are asked about current statutes, where the only alternative to the death penalty is life without parole, support for the death penalty falls off significantly.

"If you ask about death penalty vs. life in prison with restitution, support for the death penalty drops to a minority position," said Radelet. "That's in part based upon the recognition of the lack of deterrent effects and recognition of the tremendous cost of the death penalty trials."

Radelet said the cost of executing a prisoner in Florida averages about $3.2 million, mostly in trial costs. Keeping that same person in prison for life costs only about $600,000, and the millions of dollars spent on executing prisoners could be put to much better use, he said.

"If we were to ask experts for ways to reduce criminal violence," Radelet said, "they would come up with two or three dozen suggestions of programs that need increased funding and none of which would include the death penalty."

3

VIEWPOINT

"Capital punishment . . . must be used consistently in order to be effective."

A More Consistent Death Penalty Would Effectively Deter Crime

Wesley Lowe

In the following viewpoint, writer and webpage developer Wesley Lowe contends that capital punishment can be a strong deterrent to murder. Statistics prove that when the number of executions goes up, homicide rates go down; moreover, murder rates increase when there are less executions. In the United States, however, the death penalty is inconsistently applied, and most murderers realize that they are not likely to face execution. Lowe concludes that capital punishment must be administered to all death-row murderers in order for it to be a truly effective deterrent.

As you read, consider the following questions:

1. What kind of states tend to have higher crime rates, according to Lowe?
2. According to Stephen K. Layson, cited by the author, each execution deters how many murders?
3. In Lowe's opinion, how does the increase in child rape in South Africa prove that criminals are deterred by the lethal consequences of their actions?

Reprinted, with permission, from Wesley Lowe, "The Deterrent Effect of Capital Punishment," 1999 web article found at www.geocities.com/Area51/Capsule/2698/cp.html.

One argument [against capital punishment] states that the death penalty does not deter murder. Dismissing capital punishment on that basis requires us to eliminate all prisons as well because they do not seem to be any more effective in the deterrence of crime.

Others say that states which do have the death penalty have higher crime rates than those that don't, that a more severe punishment only inspires more severe crimes. I must point out that every state in the union is different. These differences include the populations, number of cities, and yes, the crime rates. Strongly urbanized states are more likely to have higher crime rates than states that are more rural, such as those that lack capital punishment. The states that have capital punishment have it because of their high crime rate, not the other way around.

The Death Penalty's Deterrent Effect

In 1985, a study was published by economist Stephen K. Layson at the University of North Carolina that showed that every execution of a murderer deters, on average, 18 murders. The study also showed that raising the number of death sentences by one percent would prevent 105 murders. However, only 38 percent of all murder cases result in a death sentence, and of those, only 0.1 percent are actually executed. On occasion, circumstances have led to meaningful statistical evaluations of the death penalty's deterrent effect. In Utah, for example, there have been five executions since the Supreme Court allowed executions to resume in 1976:

> Gary Gilmore faced a firing squad at the Utah State Prison on January 17, 1977. There had been 55 murders in that state during 1976. During 1977, in the wake of the Gilmore execution, there were 44 murders, a 20 percent decrease.
>
> A decade later, on August 28, 1987, Pierre Dale Shelby, who in 1974 forced five people to drink liquid drain cleaner, kicked a ball-point pen into the ear of one, then killed three, was executed. The count for January through August was 38 murders, a monthly average of 4.75. In the aftermath of the Shelby execution, there were 16 through the months of September to December, a monthly average of 4.0. Arthur Gary Bishop, who sodomized and killed a number of young boys, was executed on June 10, 1988. For all of 1988, there

> were 47 murders. During January–June, there were 26; for July–December, the tally was 21, a 19 percent difference.

In the wake of those three Utah executions, there have been notable decreases in both the number and the rate of murders within the state. The figures are there but abolitionists have chosen to ignore them.

Less Executions Mean More Murders

During the temporary suspension on capital punishment from 1972–1976, researchers gathered murder statistics across the country. Researcher Karl Spence of Texas A&M University came up with these statistics: in 1960, there were 56 executions in the USA and 9,140 murders. By 1964, when there were only 15 executions, the number of murders had risen to 9,250. In 1969, there were no executions and 14,590 murders, and 1975, after six more years without executions, 20,510 murders occurred. So the number of murders grew as the number of executions shrank. Spence said:

> While some [death penalty] abolitionists try to face down the results of their disastrous experiment and still argue to the contrary, the . . . [data] concludes that a substantial deterrent effect has been observed . . . In six months, more Americans are murdered than have been killed by execution in this entire century . . . Until we begin to fight crime in earnest [by using the death penalty], every person who dies at a criminal's hands is a victim of our inaction.

And more recently, there have been 56 executions in the USA in 1995, more in one year since executions resumed in 1976, and there has been a 12 percent drop in the murder rate nationwide.

And JFA (Justice for All) reports that in Texas, the highest murder rate in Houston (Harris County) occurred in 1981 with 701 murders. Since Texas reinstated the death penalty in 1982, Harris County has executed more murderers than any other city or state in the union and has seen the greatest reduction in murder from 701 in 1982 down to 261 in 1996—a 63 percent reduction, representing a 270 percent differential!

Also, in the 1920s and '30s, death penalty advocates were known to refer to England as a means of proving capital punishment's deterrent effect. Back then, at least 120 murderers

Killers Evading Punishment

Nobody can deny that there is something capricious about the way the death penalty is applied in America today. There are states, like New York, with death penalties on the books that have been cunningly written to ensure that nobody will ever actually receive a capital sentence. There are states, like Pennsylvania, where criminals are frequently sentenced to death, but where the sentences somehow are never put into effect. Even the apparent rise in executions in 1997 turns out to be a fluke. Remove one state, Texas, from the total, and the number of executions in the other 49 actually dropped below that in 1996. All together, 94 percent of the killers sentenced to death since 1976 have thus far evaded the punishment meted out to them by judge and jury.

The right way to deal with that capriciousness, however, is to ensure that the death sentence, when lawfully imposed, is promptly carried out, and not—as death-penalty critics argue—to abandon it.

David Frum, *Weekly Standard*, January 19, 1998.

---

were executed every year in the US and sometimes the number reached 200. Even then, England used the death penalty far more consistently than we did and their overall murder rate was smaller than any one of our major cities at the time. Now, since England abolished capital punishment about thirty years ago, the murder rate has subsequently doubled there and 75 English citizens have been murdered by released killers!

The Honorable B. Rey Shauer, Justice of the Supreme Court of California, has said:

> That the ever present potentiality in California of the death penalty, for murder in the commission of armed robbery, each year saves the lives of scores, if not hundreds of victims of such crimes, I cannot think, reasonably be doubted by any judge who has had substantial experience at the trial court level with the handling of such persons. I know that during my own trial court experience . . . including some four to five years (1930–1934) in a department of the superior court exclusively engaged in handling felony cases, I repeatedly heard from the lips of robbers . . . substantially the same story: "I used a toy gun [or a simulated gun or a gun in which the firing pin or hammer had been extracted or damaged] because I didn't want my neck stretched." (The penalty, at the time referred to, was hanging.)

What's more, in my state of New York, the death penalty is now in effect and there are many death penalty cases in progress, and the murder rate continues to drop faster than ever.

Consistency Makes a Difference

In 1997, in the *Atlantic*, reporter Robert Kaplan remarked that "Democratic South Africa has become one of the most violent places on earth that are not war zones. The murder rate is six times that in the United States, five times that in Russia. There are private security guards for every policeman." Yet, South African officials still insist that the death penalty won't do a thing to reduce the murder rate. The *New York Times Magazine* [reported that there has been an] epidemic of rapes of children in the country. . . .

One reason for the increase in attacks on young children is that the rapists think they are less likely to have AIDS since they know that AIDS itself has skyrocketed in Nelson Mandela's "earthly paradise." Think about that. Those rapists are less likely to attack grown women because they fear the lethal consequences of AIDS. This demonstrates that violent criminals are indeed capable of being deterred by lethal consequences for their actions if only on a sub-conscious level. If the death penalty were just as consistent, lethal, and as unstoppable as the AIDS virus, criminals would actually have reason to back down. Given the evidence, there is no logical reason to believe otherwise.

Edward Koch, former mayor of New York City, said:

> Had the death penalty been a real possibility in the minds of . . . murderers, they might well have stayed their hand. They might have shown moral awareness before their victims died . . . Consider the tragic death of Rosa Velez, who happened to be home when a man named Luis Vera burglarized her apartment in Brooklyn. "Yeah, I shot her," Vera admitted. ". . . and I knew I wouldn't go to the chair."

Making the Death Penalty Effective

Abolitionists will claim that most studies show that the death penalty has no effect on the murder rate at all. But that's only because those studies have been focused on inconsistent executions. Capital punishment, like all other applications, must be used consistently in order to be effective. However, the death penalty hasn't been used consistently in the USA for decades, so abolitionists have been able to establish the delusion that it doesn't deter at all to rationalize their fallacious arguments. But the evidence shows that whenever capital punishment is applied consistently or against a small murder rate it has always been followed by a decrease in murder. I have yet to see an example on how the death penalty has failed to reduce the murder rate under those conditions.

So capital punishment is very capable of deterring murder if we allow it to, but our legal system is so slow and inefficient, criminals are able to stay several steps ahead of us and gain leeway through our lenience. Several reforms must be made in our justice system so the death penalty can cause a positive effect.

"Higher violent crime rates [occur] in death penalty counties."

The Death Penalty Increases the Violent Crime Rate

Paul H. Rosenberg

Rather than deterring murder, the death penalty in the United States actually increases the violent crime rate, argues Paul H. Rosenberg in the following viewpoint. The author cites several studies revealing that an upsurge in murder has occurred in states and counties that reinstated capital punishment in the 1970s and 1980s. Cultures with high levels of violence and an inclination toward vengeance, he explains, experience an increased murder rate following executions—a "brutalization effect." Such is the case with the United States, the author maintains. Rosenberg is a freelance journalist.

As you read, consider the following questions:

1. According to Rosenberg, what is the average murder rate for states without the death penalty? What is the average murder rate for the thirteen states with the most executions?
2. What is the cycle-of-violence effect, according to the author?
3. The South accounts for what percentage of executions, according to the Bureau of Justice Statistics?

Reprinted, with permission, from Paul H. Rosenberg, "Bush, Gore Both Wrong on Death Penalty Deterrence," October 18, 2000, web article found at www.la-indymedia.org/display.php3?article_id=4087.

In their debate on October 17, 2000, George W. Bush and Al Gore both expressed support for the death penalty. When asked directly if they believed the death penalty served as a deterrent, both answered yes. Bush said, "I do, that's the only reason to be for it," and went on to specifically reject revenge as a justification for the death penalty. Gore said that it was "controversial," but that he believed it.

Ralph Nader, who was excluded from the debates, is opposed to the death penalty, and the facts are opposed to Bush and Gore. The thirteen states without the death penalty had an average murder rate of 3.7 per 100,000 in 1997; the thirteen states with the most executions from 1977 to 1998 (384 in all) had an average murder rate of 8.2 per 100,000—more than twice as high as the murder rate in non-death penalty states. In 1998 only one state without the death penalty had a murder rate higher than Texas, which leads the nation in executions by an enormous margin. North Dakota, without the death penalty, had a murder rate less than 1/6th of that in Texas—much like Western Europe.

A Cycle-of-Violence Effect

Of course correlation doesn't prove causation and other factors need to be considered as well. But a difference this striking in the *opposite* direction is clearly incompatible with the claim of deterrence, and strongly suggests the opposite of a deterrence effect: a cycle-of-violence effect. This consists of (1) an existing culture with high levels of violence, that actively sanctions some forms of violence (duels and other forms fighting to 'defend one's honor,' tolerance of bullying, glorification of sports involving physical aggression and hurting the opponent, etc.) (2) an actual motive of seeking revenge, consistent with the active sanctioning of violence, rationalized in terms of deterrence, (3) a brutalization effect, which results in increased murder rates as a result of executions.

Over the years there's been substantial evidence that a deterrence effect does not exist, while a cycle-of-violence effect does. Death Penalty Focus cites the Thorsten Sellin studies of the U.S. in 1962, 1967 and 1980 which concluded that the death penalty is not a deterrent. The Death Penalty Information Center cites "Four new studies on deterrence [that] throw further doubt that there is any deterrent effect from sentencing people to death or executing people for homicide. The studies did find support for a brutalization effect."

• "Capital Punishment and Deterrence: Examining the Effect of Executions on Murder in Texas" by John Sorenson, Robert Wrinkle, Victoria Brewer and James Marquart examined Texas executions from 1984 to 1997. Because of Texas's high rate of executions it provided a strongest test for the deterrent claim. However, comparing patterns in executions across the study period against the relatively steady rate of murders in Texas, the authors found no evidence of a deterrent effect. The number of executions was unrelated to murder rates or to felony rates.

• "Deterrence, Brutalization, and the Death Penalty: Another Examination of Oklahoma's Return to Capital Punishment" by William Bailey looked for a deterrent effect in murder rates and sub-type murder rates (felony-murder, argument-related killings, stranger non-felony murder, stranger robbery-related killings) in Oklahoma before and after the state resumed executions following a 25-year moratorium. Studying the period between 1989 and 1991, Bailey found no evidence for a deterrent effect, but did find a significant increase in stranger killings and non-felony stranger killings—evidence supporting a brutalization effect.

• "Effects of an Execution on Homicides in California" by Ernie Thompson examined criminal homicides in L.A. before and after California's execution of Robert Alton Harris in 1992, California's first execution after a 25-year moratorium. Thompson found slight increases in homicides during the eight months after the execution—evidence supporting a brutalization effect.

• *The Geography of Execution: The Capital Punishment Quagmire in America* by Keith Harries and Derral Cheatwood provided an extensive controlled test of the deterrence hypothesis. The authors studied differences in homicides and violent crime in 293 pairs of counties matched on the basis of geographic location, regional context, historical development, demographic and economic variables. This virtually eliminated any pre-existing cultural differences which might prime higher rates of violence. Paired counties shared a contiguous border, but differed on use of capital punishment. There was no evidence for a deterrent effect of capital punishment at the county level comparing matched counties inside and outside states with capital punishment, with and without a death row population, and with and without executions. There was evidence for a brutalization effect, however: higher violent crime rates in death penalty counties.

Brutality Generates Homicides

The brutalization effect of executions is just one facet of the more general significance of brutalization in generating homicides. In his book, *Why They Kill: The Discoveries of a Maverick Criminologist*, Richard Rhodes reports on the work of criminologist Lonnie Athens who describes a 4-stage process of violentization which is consistent with the historical brutality of pre-modern Europe and its extremely high murder rates. Since then, a centuries-long civilizing process has reduced murder rates there by 95%, while drastically reducing childhood brutalization.

A Tragic Example

In light of the many studies that have noted *increases* in murder rates in the months following an execution, we have to wonder what kind of message our nation's willingness to kill its own citizens—even its children—is sending to our young people. As Michael Godfrey of the Center on Juvenile and Criminal Justice wrote in a recent study, "The state may be tragically leading by example."

Could this be so? Are the kids in Arkansas and Kentucky and Oregon and the rest of America watching what we allow the state to do in our names and following our tragic example? When the state takes a person out of a cage where it has held them for years and kills them "to solve a problem" are the kids brutalized—even if the rest of society is too distracted or apathetic to notice?

If we are serious about reducing crime and violence in our country, then killing the death penalty is a place to begin.

Philip Brasfield, *The Other Side*, November/December 1998.

The use of corporal punishment on children—by parents as well as teachers—is gradually being outlawed in Europe, which continues to have much lower rates of murder and violent crime than the U.S. "In 1990," Rhodes writes, "when the U.S. [homicide] rate was 9.4, the British rate was only 1.5, the Netherlands 0.9, Sweden 1.5, France 1.1, Germany 1. (To anticipate one comment: The U.S. rate would have been high—4.8—even if African American offenders were excluded.)"

Rhodes also touches on the Southern culture of violence. Despite the fact that black migration to inner cities in the North and West has diffused higher murder rates throughout the country, the Death Penalty Information Center still notes "The Bureau of Justice Statistics reports that the South repeatedly has the highest murder rate. In 1997, it was the only region with a murder rate above the national rate. The South accounts for 80% of executions. The Northeast, which has less than 1% of all executions in the U.S., has the lowest murder rate."

Naturally, Southern execution patterns reflect a powerful racial bias that dominates U.S. statistics. The Death Penalty Information Center reports 158 black defendents executed for killing a white victim since 1976, compared to 11 white defendents executed for killing a black victim. (Figures updated October 10, 2000.)

Some Illuminating Questions

All this suggests that a moderator concerned with substance could have asked some very illuminating questions of the candidates. Here are just a few examples:

- "The vast majority of countries in Western Europe, North America and South America—more than 95 nations worldwide—have abandoned capital punishment. The U.S. remains in the company of countries like Iraq, Iran and China as one of the major advocates and users of capital punishment. Is this the kind of company we should keep?"
- "You say you support the death penalty because it acts as a deterrent. Can you give us one scintilla of evidence to support this claim?"
- "Western Europe has abandoned capital punishment, but has much lower murder rates than we do. Doesn't this make your deterrence argument look silly, at best?"

- “There are 22,000 homicides committed every year, while only 300 people are sentenced to death. How can this possibly be anything but arbitrary and capricious?”
- “How many millionaires have been executed in America the past 25 years? How many people who couldn’t afford their own lawyer? Is it murder we’re punishing with the death penalty, or poverty? Or race?”
- “How many millionaires on trial for murder have had their lawyers fall asleep during trial?”
- “It costs more to execute a person than to keep them in prison for life. A 1993 California study put the excess cost at $1.25 million. By themselves, executions don’t do anything to heal the pain of the families of murder victims. Wouldn’t that money be much better spent providing counseling and other immediate assistance to victim’s families undergoing severe trauma and loss?”
- “Since 1976, 158 black defendents have been executed for killing a white victim, but only 11 white defendents have been executed for killing a black victim. The Constitution originally counted blacks as 3/5ths of a white person. These figures say a black is barely more than 1/15th of a white person. How can you possibly pretend this isn’t racist? Or is the death penalty supposed to deter people from being black?”
- “Corporate crime kills far more people every year than street crime. Do you favor the death penalty for corporate officers of companies whose products, byproducts and work practices kill people? Do you favor the death penalty for *corporations* whose products, byproducts and work practices kill people? If not, can you explain to the American people why you’re so soft on crime?”
- “If cocaine cartels contributed $100 million to your campaign, would you repeal the death penalty for drug kingpins?”

VIEWPOINT

"The place where the death penalty clearly intercedes in a rational thought process is felony murder."

Executions Deter Felony Murders

William Tucker

Executions may not deter "crimes of passion"—such as arguments that escalate into murder—but they do help prevent felony homicides, contends William Tucker in the following viewpoint. A felony homicide is a murder that is committed while enacting another crime. A robber may, for example, make a calculated decision to kill his victim so that there will not be any witnesses to his crime. Twentieth-century homicide statistics clearly reveal that the death penalty deters these kinds of murders, Tucker points out. Tucker is a journalist and correspondent who writes for several conservative periodicals.

As you read, consider the following questions:

1. According to Tucker, why is it disadvantageous to use the death penalty for crimes such as robbery?
2. In the author's opinion, why did the murder rate increase sharply beginning in 1966?
3. What percentage of today's murders are "stranger murders," according to Tucker?

The death penalty has become the issue du jour. It isn't too hard to account for this. Liberals see George W. Bush as vulnerable on the issue. But Bush should be congratulated for leading a crusade against the number-one public-health and safety issue of the last 35 years: the astonishing national epidemic of felony murder. Let's be clear about what the death penalty can and can't do.

Executions probably don't deter "crimes of passion." Arguments between spouses, friends, or lovers that escalate into murder probably won't be deterred because there is no rational process leading to this sort of homicide. Tempers flare, people lose control of their emotions and strike out. At least that's what the defense attorneys tell us.

Felony Murder

The place where the death penalty clearly intercedes in a rational thought process is felony murder. This is murder committed in the course of another crime—most commonly robbery, burglary, or rape. A person who is robbing a stranger has a rational motive for killing him. The victim is the principal witness to the crime. By eliminating the victim, you eliminate the principal witness.

The decision to escalate a robbery into a murder is sometimes calculated, often impulsive. Amateur criminals are the most susceptible. A young hoodlum hijacks a car and rides around the neighborhood for half an hour trying to find a way to ditch the car's owner. He really only wants the car, but he soon realizes this person has had a long, long look at him. What other way out is there than to murder the victim? The "surprised burglar" is another common scenario. A teenager breaks into a neighbor's house and suddenly the person comes home. The kid only wants jewelry, but the neighbor knows him by sight. There isn't any chance that he isn't going to "tell." Murder is the only alternative. And in the case of a parolee or prior offender facing long years in prison, a few more years tacked on won't make much difference. Much better to chance escaping altogether. Murder is the rational choice.

For centuries, the purpose of the death penalty has been to draw a clear, bright line between felony robbery or rape and felony murder. Rape or rob and you will get a long sentence in jail. But escalate the crime into murder and the punishment becomes qualitatively different: You forfeit your life.

Well, actually, it didn't always work that well. Overzealous use of the death penalty clouded the issue. Hanging people for picking pockets produced unwanted incentives in the pickpockets. From the Enlightenment on, reformers pointed this out. "It is a great abuse among us to condemn to the same punishment a person who only robs on the highway and another who robs and murders," wrote Montesquieu in *The Spirit of the Laws* (1748). "In China, those who add murder to robbery are cut in pieces: but not so the others; to this difference it is owing that though they rob in that country they never murder. In Russia, where the punishment for robbery and murder is the same, they always murder. The dead, they say, tell no tales."

Nineteenth-century reforms brought a halt to this mistaken practice (except in the American South). A clear line was drawn between robbery and murder. The last execution in New York State took place in 1963. In the chair was a two-bit criminal who had stuck up a bar in East Harlem. When one woman didn't hand over her wallet fast enough, he put a bullet through her forehead. His execution was a clear and precise application of capital punishment. Did it work? The statistical record clearly indicates that it did.

The swift and certain application of the death penalty throughout the early years of the century brought murder into a steady decline. The peak in homicides occurred in the 1930s—generally associated with Prohibition. Executions also peaked across the country in 1935 at 200 (roughly four per state). After that point, the murder rate dropped steadily. As homicides fell, the number of executions followed them down. By the early 1960s, capital punishment was applied only in a few well-publicized cases. Still, the concept of "going to the chair" was fixed clearly in everyone's mind. By 1963, the murder rate was triumphantly low.

A Fatal Miscalculation

Then a fatal miscalculation occurred. Convinced that the problem of felony murder had been solved forever and that it was now "barbaric" to continue executions, liberals mounted a campaign to abolish capital punishment. By 1966 there was a de facto moratorium in nearly all states, and in 1971 the Supreme Court overturned all existing death-penalty laws. But at zero executions, the predictable happened. Beginning in 1966, the rate of murder skyrocketed, soaring by 1980 to more than double the 1963 rate. Moreover, this was not just a broad, general rise in murder. "Crimes of passion" stayed virtually the same. Almost the entire increase was the result of an explosion of felony murder.

Executions Deter

It is difficult to have a serious criminal justice system without a death penalty. Criminals often testify to the overpowering sense of invulnerability they feel when they attack or kill someone. "I felt like I was indestructible or invincible—like I could just do anything," confessed John Royster, accused of killing a Park Avenue dry cleaner and attacking a Central Park jogger in a 1996 spree. (His lawyers are challenging the admissibility of this statement.) Opponents of the death penalty continue to argue that there is no deterrent to the death penalty, although it is hard to see why. When executions were common in the 1940's and 50's, the murder rate was much lower. When executions stopped in the 1960's, the murder rate took off and did not start coming down until just recently.

William Tucker, *American Spectator*, March 1998.

Proving cause and effect in broad social trends is virtually impossible, and I will not try to make the case that the rejection of capital punishment was the sole cause of the upsurge in felony murders after 1966. There were many factors at work—urban riots, the broad acceptance of drugs, the general embrace of social disorder. After all, it was the Sixties. But put it this way: If the common social expectation of capital punishment indeed deterred hundreds and thousands of felony murders, and if its removal could be expected to unleash a hitherto suppressed torrent of fatal confrontations, the figures wouldn't look any different than they do in the historical record.

In 1963, 90 percent of murders were "crimes of passion."

In fact, one of the major arguments of death-penalty abolitionists was that murder had become a "crime of passion." Therefore the death penalty was "barbaric." In typical liberal fashion, the abolitionists failed to see the vast number of crimes that were being deterred by the death penalty. Once it was abolished, the furies were unleashed.

More than half of all murders are now "stranger murders"—probably the most significant social trend in the last 35 years. Fewer than half these crimes are ever solved, proving beyond any doubt that killing your victim has calculated advantages. Old-time police officers recognize the difference. "I patrolled Flatbush Avenue in the 1950s, and at least half the time when we stopped an armed robbery, the gun turned out to be unloaded," says John Coughlin, a retired New York City cop who campaigns for the death penalty. "The criminals wanted the fear of the gun, but they didn't want even the slightest possibility that the gun might accidentally go off. That meant 'going to the chair.'" Willie Sutton, the most notorious bank robber of the era, prided himself in never harming any of his victims. He had good reason.

Today, murder-in-the-course-of-a-crime has become almost routine. "Leaving no witnesses" is an articulated policy. Homicide is now the number-one cause of occupational death for women and number two (behind vehicular accidents) for men. The highest rate of victimization is among cab and livery drivers, convenience-store workers, gas station attendants, and bodega owners—people who face the public in commercial settings with little or no protection. The one ray of hope has been in the recent rise of executions. Publicizing of the death penalty seems to be penetrating the criminal mind. As executions have risen steeply in the mid 1990s, the murder rate has dropped precipitously. We are at least back to a level of 1969—still more than double the days when the death penalty was routinely enforced, but well below the peak of the execution-free 1980s. In light of this national epidemic, it is difficult to fathom why reporters and editorialists spend so much time wringing their hands over the remote possibility that somehow, somewhere an innocent person may be executed by the state. (In fact, the vast majority of overturned capital cases involve procedural technicalities and do not seriously challenge the guilt of the offender.) Still the critics persist.

In a recent dismissal of capital punishment, even in the most egregious cases, columnist Richard Cohen wrote: "The dead cannot be helped." Retrospectively, the thousands who died over the last 30 years for lack of a death penalty certainly cannot be helped. But prospectively?

VIEWPOINT 6

"Executions prevent murders, but convictions prevent even more murders."

A High Conviction Rate Is a Stronger Deterrent than the Death Penalty

Steven E. Landsburg

In the following viewpoint, Steven E. Landsburg maintains that a high conviction rate deters more murders than executions do. Potential killers are more likely to avoid murder if they face larger odds of conviction rather than smaller chances of execution. While executions do discourage homicides, they are about half as effective as convictions in preventing murders. Landsburg is the author of *Fair Play: What Your Child Can Teach You About Economics, Values, and the Meaning of Life*.

As you read, consider the following questions:

1. According to Landsburg, what kind of jackpot makes lotteries more attractive to people?
2. According to the author, what deters more crime: longer jail sentences or higher conviction rates?
3. What did Isaac Ehrlich, cited by the author, conclude about the deterrent effects of conviction versus the deterrent effects of punishment?

Reprinted, with permission, from Steven E. Landsburg, "Does Crime Pay? Yes, for Those Who Don't Wince at the Small Chance of a Big Punishment," *Slate*, December 8, 1999; found at http://slate.lycos.com/Economics/99-12-08/Economics.asp.

Criminals, by and large, must be risk-lovers—otherwise they'd be car-wash attendants instead of criminals. Lottery players, by and large, must be risk-lovers—otherwise they'd buy Treasury bonds instead of lottery tickets. You might be tempted to conclude that criminals and lottery players are often the same people. That's probably the wrong conclusion. After all, risk-lovers enjoy having all their eggs in one basket, which suggests they should pursue either crime or the lottery, but not both.

Still, if you want to understand what attracts people to crime, it pays to understand what attracts people to risky activities more generally, so it pays to understand what attracts people to the lottery.

Lotteries are attractive when they offer big prizes or (relatively) good odds. If you're running a lottery and you're going to pay out $10 million, you can offer a single $10 million jackpot or you can offer 10 prizes of $1 million each. Which is more appealing to the players? Usually, the former. For the most part, lottery players prefer a small chance of a big payout to a bigger chance of a smaller payout. That's because the people who prefer a bigger chance of a smaller payout are buying certificates of deposit, not lottery tickets. So if you want to make the lottery more attractive, it's better to double the size of the jackpot than to double the number of winners.

(More precisely, doubling the number of winners makes the lottery more attractive to the sort of person who never buys lottery tickets anyway, while doubling the jackpot makes it more attractive to the sort of person who might actually be tempted to play.)

Risk and Criminal Deterrence

Now let's apply the same reasoning to criminal deterrence. For the most part, criminals prefer a small chance of a big punishment to a big chance of a small punishment. That's because the people who prefer a big chance of a small punishment go into punishing careers like construction work or coal mining instead of crime. So if you want to make crime less attractive to criminals, it's better to double the odds of conviction than to double the severity of the punishment.

Add 10 percent to the length of the average jail sentence and crime will fall. Add 10 percent to the conviction rate instead and crime will fall even further. Like any risk-lovers, criminals are out to beat the odds, so they get particularly demoralized when the odds turn against them.

What to Do with Murder Convicts

Convicted murderers can be sentenced to lengthy prison terms, including life, as they are in countries and states that have abolished the death penalty. Most state laws allow life sentences for murder that severely limit or eliminate the possibility of parole. At least ten states have life sentences without the possibility of parole for 20, 25, 30 or 40 years, and at least 18 states have life sentences with *no* possibility of parole.

A recent U.S. Justice Department study of public attitudes about crime and punishment found that a majority of Americans support alternatives to capital punishment: When people were presented the facts about several crimes for which death was a possible punishment, a majority chose lengthy prison sentences as alternatives to the death penalty.

American Civil Liberties Union, Briefing Paper, 1996.

So much for the theory; now to the facts. What's true of the lottery should be true at the racetrack. And gambling consultant Maury Wolff confirms that if you're designing a complicated bet like a trifecta, the way to generate the most action per dollar's worth of prize money (and hence the most profit for the track) is to offer very large prizes at very long odds. Why, then, do the tracks continue to offer bets with much smaller payoffs? According to Wolff, it's because big prize winners take their money and go home while small prize winners plow their winnings back into the next race. That sets up an interesting trade-off for the track owner: One big prize maximizes profit on the current race, while several small prizes maximize the action on the next race. Interesting as that trade-off may be, it's largely irrelevant to the main point, which is that players like big prizes and long odds. (On another interesting tangent, Wolff asked me whether there's something inherently corrupt about a system where the proceeds from state lotteries are used to fund school systems that then have an incentive to produce the kind of students who will go out and play the lottery.)

Statistical Evidence

With regard to crime, let's consider the most spectacular of all crimes, murder. Here the expert is Professor Isaac Ehrlich, who, in the mid-'70s, pioneered the use of sophisticated statistical techniques to measure deterrent effects of conviction and punishment. Together with Professor Zhiqiang Liu, Ehrlich has recently revisited the subject, refuting his most vocal critics and offering new evidence in support of his original conclusion: Increase the number of convictions by 1 percent and (to a very rough approximation) the murder rate falls by about 1 percent. Increase the number of executions by 1 percent (which amounts to increasing the severity of the average punishment) and (again to a very rough approximation) the murder rate falls by about half a percent. (These numbers are based on evidence from the 1940s and 1950s. Capital punishment studies tend to focus on decades with more executions and hence more data.) As the theory predicts, convictions matter more than punishments.

That's not to say that punishments don't matter. Executions may be a less-effective deterrent than convictions, but they are nevertheless an extremely powerful deterrent; according to Ehrlich's numbers, one additional execution in 1950 could well have prevented over 20 murders. I am grateful to Ehrlich for that amazingly strong result, because I use it to illustrate three points that I'm always eager to drive home to my students. First, incentives matter, even to murderers. Second, economic theory predicts that some incentives matter more than others, and the data confirm the theory: Executions prevent murders, but convictions prevent even more murders. And finally, if you want to give policy advice, it's not enough to know your numbers. You've also got to know your values. Isaac Ehrlich, the man who proved to the satisfaction of the economics profession that capital punishment works, is a passionate opponent of capital punishment.

Periodical Bibliography

The following articles have been selected to supplement the diverse views presented in this chapter. Addresses are provided for periodicals not indexed in the *Readers' Guide to Periodical Literature*, the *Alternative Press Index*, the *Social Sciences Index*, or the *Index to Legal Periodicals and Books.*

Philip Brasfield	"The Deed That Teaches," *The Other Side*, November/December 1998.
Nat Hentoff	"The Illusion of Deterrence," *Washington Times*, November 27, 2000.
Michael Higgins	"Is Capital Punishment for Killers Only?" *ABA Journal*, August 1997.
New York Times	"Homicide Rates Are Unaffected by the Death Penalty, Study Finds," September 22, 2000.
Sean O'Malley	"The Gospel of Life vs. the Death Penalty," *Origins*, April 1, 1999.
George E. Pataki	"Death Penalty Is a Deterrent," *USA Today*, March 1997.
Bruce Ramsey	"A Difficult Road to Death," *Seattle Times*, April 16, 2000.
San Francisco Chronicle	"The Death Penalty Myth," September 27, 2000.
Andrew Peyton Thomas	"Penalty Box: A Much-Needed Reform Seem Poised to Hasten Executions—Until Federal Judges Got Their Hands on It," *National Review*, May 4, 1998.
William Tucker	"Why the Death Penalty Works," *American Spectator*, October 1, 2000.
Dale Turner	"The Death Penalty Only Serves to Further Dehumanize Society," *Seattle Times*, March 18, 2000.

CHAPTER 4

Is the Death Penalty Applied Fairly?

Chapter Preface

One of the most prevalent arguments against the death penalty is the contention that it is unfairly administered. Critics of capital punishment often maintain that minorities and the poor receive a disproportionate number of death sentences. Many point out, for example, that black defendants are more likely to receive death sentences than are whites charged with the same crime. Moreover, as Democratic congressman Jesse Jackson Jr. asserts, "the race of the victim—more specifically, whether or not the victim was white—can have an even stronger influence" on sentencing decisions in capital cases.

Statistics lend support to Jackson's claims. Researcher David Baldus, who has studied more than twenty-five hundred Georgia murder cases, discovered that defendants accused of killing whites are 4.3 times more likely to be given death sentences than those accused of murdering blacks. While fewer than 40 percent of the murder victims in Georgia are white, 87 percent of Georgia's homicide cases resulting in the death penalty involve white victims, Baldus points out. Bias is even more obvious in cases of interracial murder, reports the congressional General Accounting Office: "African Americans who murder whites are *19 times as likely to be executed* as whites who kill blacks."

Some capital punishment supporters grant that reforms are needed to prevent discriminatory applications of the death penalty. But others maintain that the claims of racial bias in sentencing decisions are based on a misreading of data. As commentator Michael Levin explains, "a white is more likely than a black to be a victim of a felony murder that carries the death sentence." Felony murder includes premeditated homicide and murder committed during the enactment of another crime such as robbery. According to Levin, blacks commit such murders at higher rates than do whites—hence the higher number of death sentences given to black defendants. When the circumstances of crimes are taken into account, he argues, it becomes clear that death penalty is imposed in a consistent manner for both whites and blacks.

In the following chapter, analysts further explore the question of whether death sentences are handed out fairly.

VIEWPOINT 1

"The likelihood of wrongful executions is less than ever."

Wrongful Executions Are Unlikely

Eugene H. Methvin

Concern about the possibility of executing the innocent has increased in recent years. In the following viewpoint, Eugene H. Methvin contends that such fears are unfounded. No one has proven that any wrongful executions have occurred, he points out. Moreover, advances in technology—such as DNA testing—are exonerating the wrongly convicted and enabling investigators to close in on perpetrators more quickly. The numerous appeals that are typically granted to state convicts also make it improbable that innocents will be executed, the author maintains. Methvin is a Washington, D.C.–based *Reader's Digest* contributing editor.

As you read, consider the following questions:

1. According to Methvin, what were the main flaws in the Bedau and Radelet study claiming that innocent people had been executed?
2. How many appeals were granted to convicted Illinois killer John Wayne Gacy, according to the author?
3. In Methvin's opinion, why is the possibility of wrongful execution *not* a good justification for abolishing capital punishment?

If there's been a change in the death-penalty winds, it's because capital-punishment opponents have been fanning a national panic over the chance that we might be putting innocent people to death. The truth is, we've never been better positioned to ascertain guilt or innocence.

In April 2000, Illinois Gov. George Ryan declared a moratorium on executions in his state. A Republican who favors capital punishment, Mr. Ryan nonetheless said Illinois had a "shameful record" of condemning innocent people to die. He based his decision in part on the case of Steve Manning, a former Chicago cop who in January 2000, became the 13th man exonerated from Illinois's death row since 1976. [The Illinois moratorium was lifted in January 2001.]

Mr. Ryan isn't the only Republican calling for a rethinking of the death penalty. In April 2000, televangelist Pat Robertson joined the American Civil Liberties Union [ACLU] in asking for a nationwide moratorium on executions. Widespread coverage has followed a new book, *Actual Innocence: Five Days to Execution and Other Dispatches From the Wrongly Convicted*, written by two lawyers and a journalist who claim DNA is proving appalling miscarriages of justice. And in May 2000, New York Gov. George Pataki proposed a state DNA review committee to examine all convictions overturned because of new genetic evidence.

Rarity of Error

Some of the scrutiny is justified. Illinois has set a national record over the past decade for convicting cops and judges in federal corruption probes, and the state has had some close calls—one death-row prisoner came within two days of execution before he was exonerated. And certainly no one can say unequivocally that no innocent person in the U.S. has been wrongly executed, or that it can't happen.

But so far no one has demonstrated that it has. Quite the opposite. With the average time consumed by appeals between sentencing and execution now at about 10 years, and with the arrival of DNA testing in the 1990s, the likelihood of wrongful executions is less than ever.

Opponents of capital punishment have pointed to the work of two abolitionist scholars, Hugo Bedau and Michael

Radelet, who claimed they found 23 instances of convicts executed between 1900 and 1986 who were later proved innocent. But only one of these executions occurred after 1976, when the Supreme Court radically revamped death-penalty procedures. Moreover, the scholars appear to have based their conclusions on defendants' briefs, newspaper stories, defense-attorney claims or lapses in prosecutor conduct or trial procedure.

Stephen Markman and Paul Cassell, two Justice Department lawyers during the Reagan administration, reviewed 13 of the 23 cases—every one since 1950, the date after which they could get original court records. Based on these actual transcripts, they demonstrated that the alleged executed innocents were "guilty as sin," and that, at least since 1950, there was no documented case of innocent individuals executed. In all 13 cases, they noted, the trial records contained eyewitness testimony, confessions, or circumstantial and physical evidence demonstrating guilt. If anything, said Mr. Markman, the Bedau-Radelet study "speaks eloquently about the extraordinary rarity of error in capital punishment."

The Roger Coleman Case

Virginia's 1992 execution of Roger Keith Coleman illustrates the point. An articulate liar and manipulator, Coleman had already served a 20-month prison term for attempted rape. Yet after an unspeakable rape-murder, he mobilized America's vocal abolitionist minority and conned the media into portraying him as the innocent victim of backwoods justice.

On March 10, 1981, Coleman went to the home of his sister-in-law, whose husband was at work, cut her throat and raped her. Blood stains on his pants, semen matching Coleman's rare blood type, and witnesses' testimony—not to mention his own lies about his movements that night—persuaded a jury to convict him.

In 1990 Kitty Behan, a former ACLU lawyer with the high-powered Washington law firm of Arnold & Porter, mounted a legal and media blitz to save him. Ms. Behan got a court order requiring a newly developed DNA test on the semen. But the highly respected expert she chose found the test pointed unmistakably to Coleman. She then hired another "expert" to dispute these findings. She issued press releases accusing another man of the murder. The man sued for libel, and Ms. Behan's law firm reportedly paid an out-of-court settlement.

Legal Protections for the Innocent

Great effort has been made in pretrial, trial, appeals, writ and clemency procedures to minimize the chance of an innocent [person] being convicted, sentenced to death or executed. Since 1973, legal protections have been so extraordinary that 37% of all death row cases have been overturned for due process reasons or commuted. Indeed, inmates are six times more likely to get off death row by appeals than by execution. And, in fact, many of those cases were overturned based on post conviction new laws, established by legislative or judicial decisions in other cases.

Justice For All, www.prodeathpenalty.com/DP.html, October, 1997.

Still, Ms. Behan's media blitz had an effect. Both *Newsweek* and *Time* ran stories portraying Coleman as an innocent victim. Neither magazine mentioned the damning DNA evidence. When U.S. District Judge Glen Williams reviewed the evidence, he declared: "This court finds the case against Coleman as strong or stronger than the evidence adduced at trial." Eleven years after he murdered his sister-in-law, Coleman was executed. But he left millions fearing an innocent man had been murdered by the justice system.

A Judicial War

Many death-row convictions are overturned not on questions of guilt but on procedural grounds, in a judicial war against the death penalty. The Georgia Supreme Court in March 2000 overturned the death sentence of a killer who nearly decapitated a former girlfriend. The court found the prosecutor had wrongly urged jurors to follow the biblical mandate: "All they who take up the sword shall die by the sword." Departing from prior decisions approving biblical arguments, Justice Norman Fletcher decreed: "Biblical references . . . improperly appeal to the religious beliefs of jurors."

Other judges have voided death sentences because jurors weren't told the killer would otherwise get life without parole.

Prosecutors, however, are forbidden to argue that killers might escape, which they do, even from high-security facilities.

Multiple appeals not only make executing the innocent more unlikely than ever, they make it hard to execute the clearly guilty. Illinois executed John Wayne Gacy in 1994 for murdering 33 young men. He had confessed, and his guilt was never in the slightest doubt. Yet his lawyers consumed 14 years with legal delays. "He had 523 separate appeals," fumes House Judiciary Chairman Henry Hyde (R., Ill.). "And none were based on a claim of innocence."

Things haven't changed much since then. On the first anniversary of the Oklahoma City bombing, Congress passed the Antiterrorism and Effective Death Penalty Act. For the first time in 128 years, legislators used their constitutional authority to strip the Supreme Court and lower federal judges of jurisdiction to hear appeals for a certain class of case.

Even under this change, a state convict can still have 10 appeals (in some cases 12), before the new law affects him. He can go through five or six state and federal courts on direct appeal, then go through them again with habeas corpus petitions. But for a second federal habeas corpus review, Congress decreed, convicts must get permission from a three-judge federal appeals panel. If he is turned down, the Supreme Court can grant only one further review, and only in rare circumstances.

As for DNA, that is doing much more than just helping re-evaluate convictions. At least 64 U.S. criminal convictions have been set aside as a result of DNA testing, according to the Innocence Project of the Cardozo Law School at Yeshiva University. But DNA testing also allows investigators to eliminate many suspects early on, and concentrate on pursuing the real perpetrators.

False Sentimentality

Even Hugo Bedau, a professor at Tufts University and a leading abolitionist, has admitted that it is "false sentimentality to argue that the death penalty ought to be abolished because of the abstract possibility that an innocent person might be executed when the record fails to disclose that such cases occur." That drunk drivers kill thousands of innocents, that airplanes fall, that pedestrians get smashed by cars, does not prevent us from drinking, flying or crossing the street. But the possibility that an innocent person may be executed is supposed to make us give up capital punishment because "death is irrevocable."

Compelled to administer justice in an imperfect world, we should not allow a utopian yearning for perfect certainty to render us moral eunuchs. As George Washington wrote a friend on the eve of the Constitutional Convention, "Perfection falls not to the lot of mortal man. We must take men as we find them."

2

Viewpoint

"The guilty will die, but occasionally so will the innocent."

Wrongful Executions Are Likely

Part I: Clarence Page; Part II: Richard Cohen

The authors of the following two-part viewpoint argue that the continued enforcement of the death penalty in the United States will likely result in the execution of innocent people. In Part I, columnist Clarence Page contends that too many wrongly convicted inmates have just barely escaped execution thanks to exonerating evidence. Such close calls provide proof that the death penalty violates American standards of decency, he points out. In Part II, columnist Richard Cohen explains that technological advances such as DNA testing do not provide relevant information about most murders and therefore cannot be relied on to prove innocence. Erroneous convictions still occur and innocent people will die unless the death penalty is abolished, he maintains.

As you read, consider the following questions:

1. According to Page, what "new spin" have death penalty supporters come up with to argue that capital punishment is fair?
2. How many inmates were released from death row between 1976 and 1999, according to Page?
3. According to Cohen, why is DNA testing not relevant for most crimes?

I

Seldom has the death penalty looked more hazardous to our national sense of decency than it does today.

Seldom have we seen so much evidence of close calls in which men have almost been executed for crimes they did not commit.

Yet, faced with the mounting evidence, death penalty defenders have come up with a new spin to argue that the death penalty is just about as fair and just as it needs to be.

It is a spin that avoids the obvious conclusion one might draw from cases like Anthony Porter, who was freed in February 1999 after spending 16 years on Illinois' death row and once came within 48 hours of execution.

An investigation by journalism students accompanied by a private investigator led to Alstory Simon of Milwaukee. Confronted with the new evidence, Simon confessed on videotape.

This is the second time an independent investigation by students of Northwestern University journalism professor David Protess has helped free someone from the state's death row. Protess' little platoon also played a pivotal role in the 1996 release of four men wrongfully convicted of a gang rape and double murder in the Chicago suburb of Ford Heights.

The New Spin

The obvious conclusion one might draw from such cases is that the death penalty poses more hazards to innocent life than it is worth.

Instead, the new spin says you should forget the obvious. The new spin says you should look at the cases of innocent inmates snatched from the jaws of the death chamber and conclude quite the opposite that, yes, the system works!

That was what a spokesman for Illinois' newly installed Gov. George Ryan said in February 1999 in rebuffing calls by death penalty opponents for a moratorium on executions.

"The process did work," David Urbanek, Ryan's spokesman, said. "Sure, it took 17 years, but it also took 17 years for that journalism professor to sic his kids on this case."

Excuse me? Is it the fault of Protess' journalism students that Porter sat so long on death row for a double murder it now appears he did not commit? Is it the fault of Porter's volunteer lawyer that the man who now has signed a confession was not charged for all that time?

That's how convoluted politicians sound when they try to put a happy face on stories of inmates who narrowly escaped execution for crimes they did not commit.

The System Does Not Work

Porter is the 76th death row inmate freed on appeal or as a result of exculpatory evidence in the United States since 1976, according to the Death Penalty Information Center in Washington.

About 30 of the 76 were assembled in a dramatic event held by death penalty opponents at Northwestern in November 1998. When some of them were asked by reporters if they thought their cases showed "the system works," they vigorously argued the opposite.

"If it was up to the system," said one, "I'd be dead."

That's the obvious conclusion, if you don't buy the government's spin.

Only Florida, where 18 inmates have been released from death row since the state reinstated capital punishment in the 1970s, has freed more inmates than Illinois, which has freed 10 in that period, including Porter, according to the center.

Those numbers do not include the cases of inmates convicted of murder who did not go to death row. Days after Porter was freed in Illinois, Anthony Gray was freed from a Maryland prison more than seven years after he was charged with first-degree murder and given two life sentences.

It was also 15 months after the real killer pleaded guilty of the crime after DNA evidence nailed him. Why the 15-month delay? "I wanted to make sure we left no stone unturned," said Calvert County State's Attorney Robert Riddle.

Right. Mistakes do happen, don't they? That simple truism is worth remembering, especially in states that try to put as many inmates as possible on a fast track to execution.

Unfortunately, the system's efforts to leave no stones unturned in locking up suspects too often exceed efforts to make sure the right person is getting locked up. The Supreme Court has made matters more hazardous in recent years by reducing the ability of death row inmates to file appeals.

The lopsidedness of the system puts a particularly tragic burden on those who are too poor to afford an adequate defense, much less the blue-ribbon lawyers hired by suspects as wealthy as, say, O.J. Simpson.

It is for that reason, the possibility of human error meting out an injustice that cannot be reversed, that I believe the death penalty falls beneath the standards a decent, fair-minded society should set for itself.

Just ask the guys who survived the close calls—and be thankful that they're still able to answer you.

II

Tinker, tinker. This is what some political figures want to do with the death penalty. Only after the accused is guaranteed a good lawyer, only after he is granted access to DNA testing, only after every safeguard is in place will these politicians and others breathe easy about capital punishment. Then they will know, to a mythical certainty, that guilty and condemned are one and the same. Who are they fooling?

Maybe themselves. Illinois Gov. George Ryan, a Republican, has suspended executions until he can be assured that only the guilty will be put to death. [This suspension ended in January 2001.] Since 1977, 13 people have been freed from Illinois' death row on account of DNA testing or other reasons. Arrested by the cops, tried by a jury, sentenced by a judge, reviewed on appeal, they just happen not to have been the people who committed the crimes. In the Senate, Patrick Leahy (D-Vt.) and Gordon Smith (R-Ore.) have jointly proposed that defendants be guaranteed competent lawyers and provided DNA testing that might prove their innocence. The Rev. Pat Robertson made a similar point when he recently called for a moratorium on executions. Capital punishment, he just noticed, discriminates against poor people who can't afford good lawyers.

Questioning the Death Penalty

Indeed, a movement is afoot to question the death penalty. One reason is a declining crime rate that has enabled politicians to suggest the once-unsuggestible. Mostly, though, the drumbeat of stories about men freed from death row on account of DNA testing has given many politicians pause—but not George W. Bush. Despite 124 executions during his [gubernatorial] administration, Bush remains a happy and cocky champion of the death penalty. In his state—and, apparently only in his state—mistakes are never made. You have his word on it.

Reprinted by permission of Rex Babin.

As a death penalty opponent, I should be the last one to scoff at this movement—but scoff I do. These suddenly skeptical politicians should understand that soon they will be off the hook. The men freed through DNA testing were mostly convicted before the procedure was available. Now, though, it is not only available but is being used to prove guilt. Soon there will be no more of those awful stories about men wrongfully convicted, years stolen from their lives and, of course, the guilty person free all that time, presumably to strike again. That era is quickly drawing to a close.

For most crimes, DNA testing is not relevant anyway. A drive-by shooting, for instance, entails no exchange of body fluids, leaves no skin under the fingernails. The only blood spilled is the victim's. If the wrong person is arrested, no DNA test will free him. Only where rape is involved is DNA testing always in order. For reasons having to do with their molecular structure, sperm cells can be isolated from other cells and used to identify the rapist—or exonerate someone falsely accused.

That leaves all other crimes, including most murders. Do the suddenly troubled believe that people are not wrongly convicted in such cases? Do they think that cops do not compel confessions and that district attorneys, convinced of guilt, do not cut some corners, withholding complicating evidence and relying on technicians who sometimes are their drinking buddies?

Are the states, especially Texas (No. 1 in executions), going to turn their systems upside down, appropriate oodles of money so that the impoverished will get an O.J. Simpson–style legal team? Will they punish defense lawyers who don't know what they're doing or who fall asleep while listening to testimony? This happens from time to time, but we are told the defendant is probably guilty anyway. Probably.

The Innocent Will Die

This is folly. DNA testing is just the latest tool in mankind's futile march to perfection in capital punishment. Every era has its scientific breakthrough—fingerprinting, blood typing, hair and fiber analysis. Still, mistakes persist. That is human nature. Most mistakes can be rectified. After an execution, that's not the case.

To want to take a life because it is considered the proportionate punishment is understandable. But to play God or be his surrogate in the face of all we know about human error is an expression of titanic arrogance coupled with a casual indifference to human life. No criminals will be deterred. Nothing will be accomplished. The guilty will die, but occasionally so will the innocent. DNA has proved that. Give it up, gentlemen. You will never get it right. You can DNA test to your heart's content, provide money for crackerjack lawyers, look every prosecutor in the eye and make him cross his heart, but the innocent will, inevitably and with certainty, die anyway. If politicians want to ensure that doesn't happen, all they have to do is abolish capital punishment. There's a test for that, too. It's called political courage.

3

VIEWPOINT

"The lesson of the DNA exonerations is not that justice triumphs in the end but that it errs quite often in the beginning."

DNA Evidence Reveals the Fallibility of Death Penalty Trials

Washington Post National Weekly Edition

In recent years, DNA evidence has been used to exonerate inmates who have been wrongly convicted of murder, note the editors of the *Washington Post* in the following viewpoint. These exonerations prove that the criminal justice system is not fool proof and that innocent people sometimes end up in prison or on death row. Post-conviction DNA tests cannot guarantee that each innocent prisoner will eventually be acquitted, the editors point out; however, such tests do shed light on the potential for error in capital trials.

As you read, consider the following questions:

1. According to the authors, what did Betty Anne Waters do to prove that her brother was innocent of murder?
2. In the authors' opinion, why is Kenneth Waters lucky?
3. What reforms would help to minimize errors during capital trials, in the authors' view?

It is tempting to see the story of Kenneth Waters, who was released from prison in Massachusetts in January 2001 after serving 18 years for a murder of which he is almost certainly innocent, chiefly as a heartwarming tale of family devotion and persistence in the face of adversity. When Mr. Waters was sentenced to life in prison for the killing of a woman named Katharina Brow, his sister—Betty Anne Waters—vowed to prove his innocence.

Ms. Waters, a high-school dropout with two children, worked her way through college and law school in order to take on his case. She reinvestigated it and located physical evidence ripe for DNA testing. She recruited the New York–based Innocence Project to help her make that testing happen. And in January 2001, the results came back, showing that somebody other than Mr. Waters is the likely killer.

The prosecution did not oppose her motion to vacate her brother's conviction and is considering whether to retry the case. Said Mr. Waters on leaving prison, "Like my mother always told me, 'Don't ever hit your sister.'"

The Lesson of the Exonerations

But Mr. Waters's case, along with other recent DNA exonerations, confronts us with more than a Hallmark moment.

Auth. © The Philadelphia Inquirer. Reprinted by permission of Universal Press Syndicate. All rights reserved.

For however strange it seems to call lucky a man who has just spent nearly two decades in jail on a bum rap, Mr. Waters is surely lucky among wrongly convicted innocents.

Had he been prosecuted in a death-penalty state, he might well be dead by now. Had his sister not devoted her life to his case, he still would be in prison. Had the physical evidence not been preserved—or had there been none to begin with, as happens in many, many cases—there would have been nothing to test.

The lesson of the DNA exonerations is not that justice triumphs in the end but that it errs quite often in the beginning—more often than can ever be proven. Reform could make such errors rarer: The accused must have serious defense lawyers available to them at trial, and state rules must be flexible enough to correct errors after the fact. But the sense of certainty that underlies capital punishment never will be justified.

Post-conviction DNA testing has allowed dozens of innocent people to walk out of prisons, but it is not a cure-all. The most these cases can offer is a window on how often the system can fail.

VIEWPOINT

"The [DNA] test's main effect will be to increase society's confidence that the man or woman being strapped to the death gurney really did commit the crime."

DNA Evidence Will Increase Public Confidence in Death Penalty Trials

Gregg Easterbrook

Since the late 1990s, DNA tests have revealed that dozens of prisoners—including death row inmates—were wrongly convicted. Many death penalty opponents believe that such DNA exonerations provide proof that capital punishment is a threat to innocents and should be abolished. In the following viewpoint, Gregg Easterbrook argues that more often than not, post-conviction DNA tests confirm an inmate's guilt. Moreover, the increased use of DNA evidence will actually convince the public that those sentenced to death are truly guilty of murder. Although DNA tests will prevent the execution of some innocents, it will also allay concerns about wrongful applications of the death penalty, the author explains. Easterbrook is a columnist for the *New Republic*.

As you read, consider the following questions:

1. What kind of crime does DNA fingerprinting help solve, according to the author?
2. According to Easterbrook, why is the American Civil Liberties Union lobbying against laws requiring felons to submit to DNA tests?

Excerpted from Gregg Easterbrook, "The Myth of Fingerprints: DNA and the End of Innocence," *The New Republic*, July 31, 2000. Reprinted by permission of *The New Republic*.

False convictions have been an important story in the year 2000. The reason? Genetic testing. So far, DNA tests have shown that at least 68 people imprisoned by state and federal courts—including some sent to death row (though none executed)—were innocent. As a result, criminal defense lawyers Barry Scheck and Peter Neufeld are spearheading a national drive to make the tests available to thousands of inmates. They have dubbed their campaign the Innocence Project—creating the impression that DNA tests will serve mainly to exonerate.

In fact, genetic evidence will serve mainly to lock people up. In England, where DNA fingerprinting was invented and has been in widespread use for a decade, law enforcement agencies have already used genetic evidence to solve some 70,000 cases. In the fairly near future, a standard item in the trunks of American police cruisers—perhaps even on each officer's belt—may be a DNA analyzer. As a suspect is arrested, police will quickly swipe the inside of his cheek with a cotton swab and pop the results into the scanner. Within minutes the machine will produce a stream of data describing the suspect's unique genetic structure. The data will be uploaded to state or national DNA databases to determine whether the suspect's DNA matches that of blood, sweat, semen, or similar bodily fluids found at the scene of unsolved crimes around the nation. Such a procedure will be good for public safety and make our legal system more just, but in the long run it will be exactly the opposite of an "innocence project"—it will result in a steady stream of inmates about whose guilt we can be almost entirely certain.

Death Penalty Opponents May Be Mistaken

The most striking effect of genetic fingerprinting may be on capital punishment, with some opponents suggesting that DNA exonerations could shift the debate in their favor. They're probably mistaken. Of the four people on Texas's death row who have been granted extra DNA testing, three have been executed anyway when genetic evidence either failed to clear them or confirmed their guilt. The fourth, Ricky McGinn, last month received a stay of execution in June 2000 from Governor George W. Bush so he too could be extended the tests—and they reportedly help support his conviction as well. The two big laboratories that process DNA tests, Cellmark Diagnostics and Forensic Science Associates, have exonerated an estimated 40 percent of the inmates whose "post-conviction" genetic evidence they have reviewed, but the other 60 percent have had their guilt confirmed—and what's being reviewed here is the genetic evidence from those with the strongest claims of mistaken conviction.

During the next few years, post-conviction DNA testing will analyze the evidence of death-row inmates convicted before genetic fingerprinting became practical, and some innocent people will surely be freed. But over time—as the system works through the backlog of those tried before genetic analysis was common—the test's main effect will be to increase society's confidence that the man or woman being strapped to the death gurney really did commit the crime. There are two basic arguments against capital punishment: that it is inherently wrong and that it might be used against the wrong person. Death-penalty opponents have been placing more and more emphasis in recent months on the second—precisely the one genetic fingerprinting will undermine.

Methods of Criminal Identification

DNA testing is not the first anti-crime device touted as infallible. Similar claims were made for fingerprinting, also developed in England, when it was introduced at the end of the nineteenth century. But criminals learned to wear gloves or to wipe the crime scene clean. What's more, because fingerprints don't readily convert into the kind of digital data that can be rapidly accessed and shared by police—searching files for a print match is laborious and expensive—regular fingerprints may solve one particular crime but are not usually much help in matching a suspect to others.

Genetic fingerprinting, however, may really allow close-to-infallible identification. In the early '80s, English geneticist Alec Jeffreys realized that the "markers" on human chromosomes—short, structural areas of the genome—are unique from person to person, except for identical twins. Jeffreys developed a test that converts gene markers into a readout similar to a bar code, which can be easily loaded into computers. Not only has the Jeffreys test proved extremely reliable in identifying individuals, but, because it generates a digital result, computers can cross-reference one genetic fingerprint with thousands or millions of others, quickly and cheaply linking suspects to past crimes. In recent years, DNA-fingerprinting technology has advanced to the point that, rather than requiring a good sample of blood or semen—which often meant securing warrants to jab suspects with needles—a speck of sweat or a swab from the inside of the mouth will do the trick. A test of mitochondrial DNA—which, while not unique to each individual, tells whether the DNA comes from a particular family's maternal line—can even be conducted on a strand of hair or "degraded" blood and bodily fluid samples that have been kept in storage. The cost of DNA fingerprinting has also dropped dramatically, from about $5,000 when the tests were first developed to about $100 for the newest versions, and is still falling.

The DNA Fingerprint

In recent years, scientists have learned how to identify an individual by his or her genetic makeup, as encoded by deoxyribonucleic acid (DNA). Every person has a unique configuration of DNA, and that code is imprinted on each cell in the human body. Police often gather bodily materials such as hair, semen, blood or fingernails at a crime scene, since those materials can be analyzed to determine whether the "DNA fingerprint" of a person accused of a crime matches the DNA samples recovered at the crime scene. If the defendant's DNA does not match that found at the crime scene, it becomes more difficult to prove that he or she was involved in the crime.

Issues and Controversies on File, September 15, 2000.

Though very reliable, DNA fingerprinting won't solve every crime. It is useful mainly for what might be called intimate violent crimes, in which the perpetrator struggles with the victim and leaves behind blood, semen, or something else testable. (In the recent controversy over George W. Bush's execution of Gary Graham, for instance, genetic evidence was moot—the victim was shot from a distance, leaving nothing of the killer's to test.) At other times, DNA in itself may neither exculpate nor damn. A hair from the murderer of Ricky McGinn's twelve-year-old stepdaughter was found on her corpse, for instance, and a DNA test is believed to show that this hair came from either McGinn or a close maternal relative of his. So, although a prosecutor could not convict McGinn on the DNA evidence alone, it could be a critical component of a larger case.

While there is currently no way to beat a DNA test, that could change, especially if criminals grow more careful with bodily fluids—say, abandoning knives for guns shot from afar. And people won't be researching biotech just to cure diseases—perhaps some enterprising chemist will invent a pill that scrambles the genetic markers in sweat and semen. But for now, at least, genetic fingerprinting is just shy of foolproof. . . .

Fears About DNA Fingerprinting

Yet, for routine police work, many states actually forbid DNA fingerprinting or, nonsensically, allow it only after crimes of extreme violence—as though violent criminals should be caught but not mere thieves or carjackers. . . . Fighting efforts to more effectively use genetic evidence is the American Civil Liberties Union (ACLU), which is lobbying against testing laws [requiring convicted felons to submit to DNA analysis] on the grounds that chromosome material deserves privacy protection because it might reveal such things as sexual orientation.

Why a murderer has a right to sexual privacy (or any kind of privacy) isn't clear, but in any case the ACLU claim evinces confusion about what Jeffreys-style DNA tests can show. The "markers" analyzed in police tests constitute only a small, structural part of the genome. Just as a traditional fingerprint doesn't tell you anything about the suspect's personality—it just tells you about the shape of his or her finger ridges—genetic markers don't reveal anything about IQ or disease disposition or sexual orientation. Analyzing such complex traits, assuming it can be done at all, would require far more sophisticated tests, along the lines of the years-long human genome initiative. Perhaps someday there will be a quick, cheap test that gives police personal information derived from genes; that may be a reason to enact legal safeguards. For now, the main reason the ACLU seems to fear DNA fingerprinting is that it works.

And that should give death-penalty opponents pause as well. Expanded use of DNA evidence will free a few death-row innocents, which would be a blessing. But the new technology will also make society much more confident that those receiving their last meals really are guilty of a mortal sin. Suspicions that the innocent are being executed will not grow stronger as DNA testing spreads—they will grow weaker. And so opponents of capital punishment will lose the offensive they have claimed in recent months. They will be forced back to their real argument, the one that technology can't undermine: the inherent wickedness of execution itself.

5

VIEWPOINT

"Both the race of the defendant and the race of the victim matter when it comes to death sentences."

The Death Penalty Is Discriminatory

Part I: Mark Costanzo; Part II: Friends Committee on National Legislation

In Part I of the following two-part viewpoint, Mark Costanzo argues that the death penalty is arbitrary and discriminatory. Murderers of whites are more likely to receive the death penalty than are murderers of blacks, he points out, and the poor—who generally receive substandard legal assistance—are executed more often than the rich. Costanzo is the author of *Just Revenge: Costs and Consequences of the Death Penalty*. In Part II, the Friends Committee on National Legislation, a Quaker lobbying group, compares two similar murder cases to see if racial bias influenced sentencing. They discover that the race of the victim determined whether the prosecutors sought a life sentence or the death penalty.

As you read, consider the following questions:

1. According to Costanzo, who has the best chance of avoiding the executioner?
2. What happens to the majority of death row inmates, according to Costanzo?
3. According to the Friends Committee, how much more likely are blacks to receive a death sentence in comparison to non-blacks?

Part I: Reprinted, with permission, from Mark Costanzo, "How Murderers Can Avoid the Executioner," *The San Diego Union-Tribune*, January 14, 1998. *Part II:* Reprinted from "The Death Penalty: Is It Arbitrary, Capricious, and Racially Skewed?" editorial in *FCNL Washington Newsletter*, June 20, 2000, by permission of the Friends Committee on National Legislation.

I

The impending execution of Karla Faye Tucker in Texas has received national attention for the simple reason that she is a she. The 37 men Texas sent to the death chamber in 1997 rated barely a mention outside the Lone Star state. Tucker will become the first woman executed in Texas since the Civil War and the first woman killed in any U.S. execution chamber since 1984. [Tucker was executed in February 1998.]

Because judges, juries and governors are squeamish about killing women, female murderers are seldom sentenced to death. Even when they are sentenced to death, they tend to have their sentences commuted to life imprisonment. Clearly, being female is one good way to avoid the executioner—but there are several others.

How to Escape the Executioner

Another good way to improve the odds of escaping the executioner is for a murderer to make sure that his victim is African-American. Those who kill white people are more than four times as likely to be sentenced to death than those who kill black people.

If the murderer is white, the odds are even better. A black murderer whose victim is white is the most likely to end up in the execution chamber, while a white murderer whose victim is black has the best chance of avoiding the executioner. Since the death penalty was restored in 1976, only six white people have been executed for murdering a black person, while 112 black people have been executed for murdering whites.

Probably the simplest way to escape the executioner is to be rich. Discrimination against the poor is especially blatant when it comes to deciding who lives and who dies. As the late U.S. Supreme Court Associate Justice William O. Douglas put it, "one searches our chronicles in vain for the execution of any member of the affluent strata of this society."

Although poor defendants on trial for murder are entitled to a lawyer, they are not necessarily entitled to a good lawyer. The poorly trained, poorly paid court-appointed lawyers who usually represent poor defendants are usually no match for experienced prosecutors who can rely on the investigative skills of local police. Not surprisingly, defendants represented by court-appointed attorneys are more than twice as likely to be sentenced to death than those represented by private attorneys or public defenders.

But even if you're a penniless African-American male and your victim is white, your odds of escaping the executioner are still quite good. In 1997 74 prisoners were executed in the United States—a 42 year high, that amounts to less than one half of one percent of the total number of people who commit murders each year. And we have never killed more than a small percentage of murderers—the execution rate peaked in 1938 when just over 2 percent of murderers were executed.

To provide further perspective, consider that each year we add about 300 inmates to the 3,200 people who are already waiting for their appointment with the executioner. Even if we begin killing 100 inmates every year, we will never eliminate the backlog. The vast majority of death row inmates will not die at the hands of the executioner. Some will have their convictions overturned, many will have their sentences changed to life imprisonment without parole, many will die in prison of natural causes.

The too-often-overlooked truth is that it has never been difficult to evade the executioner. Our system of capital punishment has long been little more than an elaborate, costly charade.

We seldom send prisoners to the execution chamber, and when we do, we routinely discriminate on the basis of race, wealth and gender. It is time to abandon the discriminatory charade of capital punishment and to expand the public discourse on crime and punishment.

II

"Three Employees Slain at D.C. McDonald's," *Washington Post*, August 5, 1995. As the manager and three workers were closing up for the night, another McDonald's employee arrived. Once inside, the man forced the manager, at gunpoint, to open the safe, then shot and killed the manager and two workers. A third worker survived when the gun failed to fire.

"Three Employees Killed at D.C. Starbucks," *Washington*

Post, July 8, 1997. A Starbucks' employee, arriving for work, found the bodies of the night manager and two co-workers. All three had been shot. Attempted robbery is believed to have been the motive.

An Arbitrary Punishment

Who receives the death penalty has less to do with the violence of the crime than with the color of the criminal's skin or, more often, the color of the victim's skin. Murder—always tragic—seems to be a more heinous and despicable crime in some states than in others. Women who kill and who are killed are judged by different standards than are men who are murderers and victims.

The death penalty is essentially an arbitrary punishment. There are no objective rules or guidelines for when a prosecutor should seek the death penalty, when a jury should recommend it, and when a judge should give it. This lack of objective, measurable standards ensures that the application of the death penalty will be discriminatory against racial, gender, and ethnic groups.

Jesse Jackson Sr. with Jesse Jackson Jr., *Legal Lynching: Racism, Injustice and the Death Penalty*, 1996.

These two cases were strikingly similar. One might have expected them to have been prosecuted similarly. They were not. The differences illustrate some of the arbitrary and capricious elements of the criminal justice system and, perhaps, the influence of race.

Similar Crimes, Different Outcomes

The worker apprehended in the McDonald's case, Kenneth Joel Marshall, was charged in a 25-count indictment that included first-degree murder. The assistant U.S. attorney in charge of the case sought a sentence of life without parole.

The suspect apprehended in the Starbucks' case, Carl Derek Cooper, was charged in a 48-count indictment that included first-degree murder, as well as charges for other crimes committed between 1993 and 1997. These additional charges led the U.S. attorney to prosecute under federal (rather than D.C.) law, though she did not seek the death penalty. However, in a move that became highly publicized and much-criticized, Attorney General (AG) Reno overruled the U.S. attorney and insisted on seeking the death penalty.

Many D.C. residents, death penalty opponents, civil rights activists, and others were quick to point out salient differences between the McDonald's and Starbucks' cases. Although both Marshall and Cooper are black, the McDonald's slayings occurred in southeast D.C., where most residents are black and all three victims were black. The Starbucks' killings occurred in Georgetown, a well-to-do, predominantly white district and two of the three victims were white.

AG Reno defended her decision to seek the death penalty against Cooper on the basis of his cumulative record. However, she did not convince many of her critics. D.C. Delegate Eleanor Holmes Norton asserted that "It's the focus of the press, it's the downtown location, it's the race of some of the victims that gets the death penalty imposed."

Racial Disparities in Death Penalty Application

The differences in handling the two cases have fueled the debate about fairness in the application of the death penalty. The racial overtones bolster the arguments of those who maintain that the death penalty is applied in a racially-disparate manner.

Death penalty critics have long charged that the discretion given to prosecutors to decide whether or not to seek the death penalty leads to arbitrary and capricious application of the death penalty. Many critics also hold that the racism prevalent in U.S. society pervades all elements of the criminal justice system (police, prosecutors, judges, and juries) and leads to disparate treatment of black persons and white persons. Documenting racism is difficult. Easy-to-compile statistics (such as the race of death-row inmates or the proportion of racial minorities prosecuted under federal death penalty statutes) fall short because they fail to consider the entire pool of death-eligible prisoners, to analyze the nature of the crime, or to consider mitigating and aggravating circumstances. However, David Baldus and colleagues recently published a well-designed study of death penalty application in the city of Philadelphia between 1983 and 1993.

Baldus et al. found that both the race of the defendant and

the race of the victim matter when it comes to death sentences. With respect to the race of the defendant, in jury penalty-trial decisions, black defendants even at low culpability levels (where substantial mitigating factors were present) received death penalty sentences, whereas non-black defendants were sentenced to death only at very high culpability levels (where aggravating factors far outweighed mitigating factors). Moreover, at high culpability levels, black defendants were more likely to be sentenced to death than were non-black defendants. Overall, black defendants were nearly three times as likely to receive a death sentence than were non-black defendants.

With respect to the race of the victim, a sentence of death was more likely to be imposed in cases where the victim was non-black than in cases with black victims, regardless of culpability level. Overall, a jury was one and a half times more likely to sentence a defendant to death when the victim was non-black than when the victim was black.

The results of the Philadelphia study may not apply to all jurisdictions in the U.S. However, it is likely that many cities and states have similar or worse records.

Arbitrary, capricious, and racially-disparate sentencing can be reduced. But there is no way to ensure complete fairness in the application of the death penalty except by ending it.

"When looking at the circumstances consistent with capital crimes, we find no evidence of racial bias."

The Death Penalty Is Not Discriminatory

Dudley Sharp

In the following viewpoint, Dudley Sharp argues that the death penalty is not applied in a racially biased manner. He asserts that skewed and exaggerated statistics have led many to conclude that racism is the reason that blacks are more likely than whites to be sentenced to death and that murderers of whites are the most likely to be executed. In actuality, Sharp explains, whites are most often the victims of felony murders that are punishable by the death penalty, and blacks commit such felonies at a higher rate than do whites. Sharp is the vice president of Justice For All, a Texas-based victims' rights group.

As you read, consider the following questions:

1. According to Sharp, what percentage of imprisoned U.S. murderers are black?
2. In comparison with blacks, how much more likely are whites to be executed for committing murder, according to the author?
3. What is the real determining factor for sentencing in murder cases, according to Sharp?

I don't know about you, but when I get into a discussion about the death penalty, my first thoughts go to the victim and to the brutality of the murder. That is the foundation of the just nature of the death penalty. Too often these days, however, the death penalty is discussed in different terms. Inevitably, with the racial history of this country, the effect of race in the application of the death penalty has become a central part of the death-penalty discourse. This is particularly true as some politicians are making the case for a death-penalty moratorium, in part to consider whether the death penalty is inherently racist.

All too often, however, those arguments are spurious. In the death penalty debate, it should be the facts, and not the hype, that are in black and white.

A Closer Look at the Statistics

Often such discussion begins with the obvious: the race of the defendant. The Death Penalty Information Center (DPIC) reports that black murderers represent 35% of those executed, white murderers 56%. As the argument goes, this must be evidence of systemic racism, as blacks represent 12% of the population, whites 74%.

Fortunately, the United States does not execute people based on their population counts but on the murders they commit. As blacks represent 47% of murderers and whites 37%, we see that whites are twice as likely to be executed for committing murder as are their black counterparts. Furthermore, the Bureau of Justice Statistics says that whites sentenced to death are executed 17 months more quickly than blacks.

With 98% of all head prosecutors in the United States being white, according to DPIC, how is such a result possible? Maybe prosecutors, judges and juries are focusing on the crimes and not the race of the defendant. That is not the case, say anti-death penalty groups, such as Amnesty International, and now the United Nations. If you adjust for the specific aggravating factors present within capital crimes, you find clear evidence of racism.

Death-penalty opponents note, for example, that the Supreme Court, in the famous race-based challenge to the death penalty (*McCleskey v. Kemp*), found in 1987 that those who murderer whites were 4.3 times more likely to be sentenced to death than those who murder blacks, under similar circumstances. Dr. David Baldus, who did the statistical study on McCleskey's behalf, also completed a recent study in Philadelphia where it was reported to show that black murderers were four times more likely to receive a death sentence than white murderers.

With such results, how can anyone dispute the racist application of the death penalty? Quite easily. The Supreme Court, as well as many others, confused odds with multiples. The data reflect odds of 4-to-1, not four times more likely.

What difference does it make? In Baldus' Philadelphia study, we find that if only 2% more white murderers had been sentenced to death and only 2.5% fewer black murderers had been sentenced to death, then each group would have been sentenced to death by juries at the same rate—a far cry from the 400% differential stated within the incorrect interpretation of "four times"!

A Punishment That Fits the Crimes

The next issue raised is the victim's race. While blacks and whites comprise about an equal number of murder victims, the ratio of white-to-black victims in death-penalty cases is about 7-to-1. This has given rise to the allegation that the "system" only cares about white murder victims.

A horrible accusation, if true. However, the ratio of white-to-black victims in the aggravated circumstances necessary for a capital murder conviction (rape, robbery, carjacking, burglary, police murders, serial/multiple murders, etc.) is from 4-to-1 to 8-to-1—numbers consistent with the victim ratios on death row.

The final resting place for the racism charge lies within those cases where blacks have been executed for murdering whites and whites have been executed for murdering blacks. There have been 144 blacks and 10 whites executed under such circumstances, or a ratio of 14-to-1.

As blacks are about 2.5 times more likely to murder whites than the other way around, there appears to be a huge disparity in such executions. Is racism the reason?

If we look at robbery, the aggravated crime found most often in capital cases, we find that when there is a robbery with injury, the ratio of black robbers/white victims versus white robbers/black victims is 21-to-1. Again, when looking at the circumstances consistent with capital crimes, we find no evidence of racial bias. The determining factor for sentencing in death-penalty cases is what it should be—the aggravating nature of the crimes. Both the Rand Corp. study of 1991 and the research presented by Smith College professors Stanley Rothman and Stephen Powers in 1994 confirm that finding.

Sheer Propaganda

The notion that inmates on death row are usually poor African-Americans is sheer propaganda. There are more whites than blacks on death row. Each year more whites than blacks are executed. If there was a shocking racial disparity anywhere, it is not in the punishing but in the committing of murder: Blacks comprise only 12 percent of the population, yet 50 percent of all homicides are committed by blacks.

Jeff Jacoby, *Conservative Chronicle*, May 28, 1997.

In other words, it appears that any racial variations present within the data are reflective of the crimes themselves and not racial bias within the system. A review of those studies, as well as of criminal-justice statistics, within the context of the aggravating circumstances present within capital murders and the related statutes, produces the same conclusion.

Making Reasoned Judgments

There will always be some variables of race, ethnicity and class within any study of criminal-justice practices, and based on historic, as well as current prejudices, we can never lower our guard. Because all studies are subject to poor protocols, bias and misinterpretation, we must make reasoned judgments based on as many respected considerations as we may have at our disposal.

And even if criminal-justice statistics did not show the obvious correlation between crimes and the application of the death penalty, we should note what the Supreme Court stated in *McCleskey*: "Where the discretion that is fundamental to our criminal justice process is involved, we decline to assume that what is unexplained [by measured factors] is invidious."

Sound ideas should not be eliminated based on misguided statistics. In the case of the death penalty, the facts lead to only one conclusion. No moratorium is necessary.

7

VIEWPOINT

"This ultimate sanction should not be applied to those who lack the mental capacity to understand fully the consequences of their own actions."

The Retarded Should Not Receive the Death Penalty

Rodney Ellis and Joseph Fiorenza

It is wrong to execute the mentally retarded, argue Rodney Ellis and Joseph Fiorenza in the following viewpoint. Since mentally retarded criminals are incapable of understanding the consequences of their actions, they should be exempt from the death penalty. Capital punishment should be reserved only for those who have the intellectual capacity to be morally accountable, the authors maintain. Ellis is a Democratic state senator in Texas. Fiorenza is the bishop of the Catholic diocese of Galveston and Houston, Texas.

As you read, consider the following questions:

1. What was the 1989 U.S. Supreme Court ruling on mental retardation and capital cases, according to Ellis and Fiorenza?
2. According to a poll cited by the authors, what percentage of Texans opposes the death penalty for the mentally retarded?
3. Why are child murderers not executed, according to the authors?

Reprinted, with permission, from Rodney Ellis and Joseph Fiorenza, "Criminal to Be Executing Mentally Retarded Inmates," *Houston Chronicle*, May 3, 1999.

Limmie Arthur believed that he was sentenced to death because he couldn't read. He diligently tried to learn so he could earn his general equivalency diploma because he thought he would get a reprieve if he was successful. Morris Mason asked a legal aid attorney what he should wear to his funeral because he couldn't understand that he would not be alive after his execution.

The fact that both of these inmates were mentally retarded and had functional IQs of no more than 65 had no bearing on their fate—both were executed by their respective states.

Dozens of others like them have been put to death in our prisons, in some states with no more evidence to convict them than their own childish confessions.

In 1999, the Texas Senate's Criminal Justice Committee passed SB 326, which would prohibit a court from sentencing a defendant to death if the court found that the defendant was mentally retarded. [This bill did not pass into law.]

The amazing thing is not that the Legislature considered this bill; it is that the Legislature even had to consider it. It is past time for Texas to wipe this shameful, inhumane behavior from its law books.

In 1989, the United States Supreme Court ruled that mental retardation and mental disabilities may constitute mitigating circumstances in capital sentencing and evidence of its existence must be permitted in jury deliberations.

The court left it open to the states and the federal government to ban the practice. Although Congress and 12 of the 40 death-penalty states have prohibited the execution of people with mental retardation, Texas has done nothing.

An Excessive Punishment for the Retarded

This bill is not about the death penalty. Frankly, we disagree about capital punishment. One of us, (Sen. Ellis) supports it, while the other (Bishop Fiorenza) and his fellow Texas bishops oppose it. But we agree on one thing: This ultimate sanction should not be applied to those who lack the mental capacity to understand fully the consequences of their own actions.

Many Texans agree with us. A Texas poll showed that, while most support the death penalty, over 73 percent of

Texans are opposed to execution of the mentally retarded. As the most extreme sanction available to the state, the death penalty should be reserved for an offender who has the highest degree of moral culpability for a crime. As the polls show, Texans recognize that executing persons with mental retardation is disproportionate and excessive because mentally retarded individuals simply lack the ability to act as the most hardened, calculating offenders.

We do not want to suggest that people with mental retardation should not be punished when they break the law, nor do we think that people with mental retardation are not responsible for their actions. We simply believe that when the state uses its ultimate legal power—the power to take away life—we must be careful that it is reserved for those with the highest degree of blameworthiness. Can we be sure that a person with limited intelligence, incapable of even understanding his or her own actions, had that degree of culpability? Of course not.

The Compassionate Thing to Do

If the death penalty is to be maintained, it should clearly be limited to the most vicious, premeditated crimes. The acts of mentally disadvantaged criminals clearly do not qualify. This distinction can be recognized by introducing verdicts of "guilty but mentally ill" and "guilty but mentally retarded," which would prohibit the death penalty in such cases and automatically impose sentences of life without the possibility of parole. This would offer some measure of protection to the mentally disadvantaged while guaranteeing the protection of the public. This is clearly the most logical and compassionate thing to do.

Michael B. Ross, *Humanist*, January/February 1999.

As a society, we already recognize this. That is why we do not execute children, even when the news brings us horrific stories of violence by sometimes very young children. Why is that? It is because we recognize that judgment and responsibility can only come with intellectual capacity and experience. Children aren't held to a moral standard beyond their intellectual capacity.

The Legislature faces a daunting task. In a state that is

hard on crime and harder on criminals, the temptation is to wash our hands of these lives we are ending. As citizens, moral courage and civic duty require us to speak out for what is right, no matter how politically unpopular or difficult it may seem. Moreover, prohibiting the execution of mentally retarded offenders protects ourselves by ensuring against the spectacle of killing individuals who do not truly comprehend their punishment.

Virtually every group that has expertise in the area of mental retardation, including the American Association on Mental Retardation, the oldest and largest professional organization of mental retardation in the country, opposes the execution of persons with mental retardation. The American Bar Association House of Delegates has stated that mentally retarded persons should be spared, not because of any sympathy for their plight, but because the integrity of the criminal justice system would be eroded if persons with a lack of understanding of what is happening to them are executed.

Twelve states and the federal government have concluded that executing people with mental retardation does not serve justice. It is our hope that Texas will be next to join this national trend and put an end to this inhumane practice.

VIEWPOINT

"Responsibility in the criminal justice system is based on moral blameworthiness, not intellectual achievements."

The Retarded Should Not Be Exempt from the Death Penalty

Cathleen C. Herasimchuk

In the following viewpoint, Cathleen C. Herasimchuk argues against a proposed Texas statute that would prohibit the execution of murderers having an IQ of 65 or less. She contends that a person with limited intellectual capacity may still know right from wrong, and that juries should be allowed to decide when a mentally retarded murderer is morally culpable for his crime. Setting an IQ standard of 65 would simply encourage criminals to score poorly on such tests to evade death sentences, she points out. Herasimchuk, a former Harris County, Texas, assistant district attorney, is a lawyer in private practice in Houston, Texas.

As you read, consider the following questions:

1. In Herasimchuk's opinion, how should society judge the moral blameworthiness of an act?
2. How many states prohibit the execution of the mentally retarded, according to the author?
3. In the author's view, what are the four main problems with the proposed Texas statute that would forbid the execution of murderers with low IQs?

Reprinted from "Keep Inmates' IQs Out of Death Penalty Decisions," by Cathleen C. Herasimchuk, *Houston Chronicle*, May 21, 1999. Reprinted with permission of the author.

The Texas Legislature is presently poised to pass another one of those "do-good" humane-sounding statutes that ends up wreaking havoc in the criminal justice system.

The Senate has passed, and the House is about to vote on, a statute that will ban the death penalty for anyone who commits a capital murder but is mentally retarded. The argument goes: "We don't execute sixth graders, so we shouldn't execute a person with a sixth grade intelligence." It sounds great. It is muddle-headed and will cause untold mischief in our criminal justice system. [The proposed statute eventually failed.]

First, it is a fallacious argument. The execution of children is not prohibited because we believe that they, as a class, have low IQs. They don't.

We prohibit the execution of children because they do not have the years of experience, adult guidance, social development and spiritual training to fully understand and appreciate moral choices.

Is the Texas Legislature saying that Forrest Gump, no intellectual giant, was also a moral midget, incapable of sorting out right and wrong? Many thought the movie's message was the opposite.

Moral Culpability

Responsibility in the criminal justice system is based on moral blameworthiness, not intellectual achievements. Moral culpability is composed of much more than sheer IQ. This proposed statute, however, adopts a definition of mental retardation that relies almost exclusively upon a numerical IQ test. We used to measure the culpable moral blameworthiness of an act by the entirety of a person's state of mind: his factual knowledge, intellectual understanding, intent, his spiritual and moral development. In sum, his full character and background.

Second, the Texas Legislature used to, and the United States Supreme Court still does, trust the jurors in these cases to determine whether the mental retardation, mental illness or any other possible mitigating factor calls for a sentence less than death. No more. Apparently, Texas jurors cannot be trusted with that decision and discretion any more. The Legislature notes that some 74 percent of Texans believe that mentally retarded persons should not be executed. Good. Those Texans are on juries. They can, should and currently do exercise that belief in appropriate cases.

The sponsors of this bill note that 12 other states (out of 42 states that permit capital punishment) have implemented a blanket prohibition against imposing the death penalty upon those capital murderers who are mentally retarded. Thus, we must follow those states lockstep. There is no suggestion that any Texas jury has ever gotten it wrong and imposed the death penalty upon a mentally retarded person inappropriately or unfairly. The sponsors point to not one single example of injustice by a Texas jury that must be corrected.

The Problem with the Proposed Statute

What, specifically, is wrong with this statute? First, the bill sets up a presumption that a capital murder defendant with an IQ test of 65 or less is mentally retarded. Once this test result is introduced to a judge in a pretrial hearing, a jury cannot even consider the death penalty for this defendant unless the state can offer enough evidence to rebut that test. No one has any idea how the state could do that.

Neither the judge nor a prosecutor can make the defendant "try hard" on another IQ test. Indeed, why would a capital murder defendant ever try to do well on an IQ test if he knew he was exempt from a possible death sentence if he did poorly? One seasoned district attorney told the Senate Committee that the day after this bill was passed, the collective IQ of death row would drop a thousand points. He was called cynical. He was realistic. When faced with the choice between death or doing poorly on a test, who would not choose self-preservation? The judge does not even have the authority to order the defendant to take another test.

Second, how would the judge know if the defendant's test result is reliable? He won't. There are no guidelines in the bill concerning who is competent to administer or interpret the test. What if the defendant took five IQ tests, scored in the 70s and 80s in four of them, but scored 64 on one of them? Can he offer only the lowest one and hide the rest? No one knows. Suppose the defendant's IQ tests from childhood and youth were all above 65, but his post-arrest test is below 65. The bill is concerned only with the defendant's mental retardation at the time of the capital murder, so would the earlier tests be inadmissible? Sufficient to rebut the present test? The bill does not say.

Third, the bill does not say what type of evidence would rebut the defendant's "under 65" test result. The sponsors of this bill have not set out or suggested any rebutting evidence.

Mental Retardation and the Death Penalty

Some contend that laws protecting the mentally retarded from the death penalty open the way for an inmate with even slightly below-average intelligence to use his or her mental capacity as an excuse for murder. In a case in Arkansas, convicted murderer Barry Lee Fairchild, 41, was denied clemency, even after his lawyers charged that he was mentally retarded. According to his lawyer, Fairchild had an I.Q. of 60 to 80, "depending on who gives the test and when." (I.Q. stands for intelligence quotient, a test used to measure general knowledge and comprehension. A normal I.Q. is 100.)

Although Arkansas law forbids the execution of defendants with an I.Q. of 65 or lower, Judge Thomas Eisele said there was insufficient evidence that Fairfield had such a low mental capacity. Fairchild was executed by lethal injection on August 31, 1995.

Issues and Controversies on File, December 29, 1995.

Fourth, under this bill, the prosecution is not even entitled to advance notice that the defendant will offer pretrial evidence of mental retardation. The bill permits trial by ambush and will demand a battle of the experts. The already slow process in capital murder cases will creep even slower, if at all.

An Ill-Conceived Approach

If we believe that those with a low IQ are never sufficiently blameworthy to permit a sentence of death, what about those with a serious mental illness who are nonetheless sane at the time of the capital murder? Surely they deserve the same blanket protection as those with a low IQ. If jurors cannot be trusted to determine the moral culpability of those who are mentally retarded, surely they cannot be trusted when it comes to those who are mentally ill. Or is this bill the first step down the road to taking the capital murder sentencing decision away from Texas jurors entirely?

This bill sounds deceptively good. Who could possibly be in favor of executing the mentally retarded? According to the bill's author, only the "bloodthirsty." But the road to chaos in the criminal justice system is paved with good intentions and a warm heart. Until and unless the Texas Legislature determines that Texas jurors cannot fairly and appropriately assess moral blameworthiness in individual cases, the Legislature should not take such an ill-conceived, blunderbuss approach. If it's not broken, don't wreck it.

Periodical Bibliography

The following articles have been selected to supplement the diverse views presented in this chapter. Addresses are provided for periodicals not indexed in the *Readers' Guide to Periodical Literature*, the *Alternative Press Index*, the *Social Sciences Index*, or the *Index to Legal Periodicals and Books*.

Craig Aaron	"Criminal Injustice System," *In These Times*, December 27, 1998.
Alan Berlow	"Lethal Injustice," *American Prospect*, March 27–April 10, 2000.
Walter Berns and Joseph Bessette	"Why the Death Penalty Is Fair," *Wall Street Journal*, January 9, 1998.
Raymond Bonner and Sara Rimer	"Executing the Mentally Retarded Even as Laws Begin to Shift," *New York Times*, August 7, 2000.
Fox Butterfield	"New Study Adds to Evidence of Bias in Death Sentences," *New York Times*, June 7, 1998.
Richard Cohen	"One Fatal Mistake Not Made," *Washington Post*, February 15, 2001.
Ann Coulter	"O.J. Was 'Proved Innocent,' Too," *Human Events*, June 20, 2000.
Ronald Dworkin	"The Court's Impatience to Execute," *Los Angeles Times*, July 11, 1999.
Gregg Easterbrook	"DNA and the End of Innocence," *The New Republic*, July 31, 2000.
Bob Herbert	"Dead Wrong," *New York Times*, February 1, 2001.
Robert L. Jackson	"Study Finds Racial Gap on Death Row," *Los Angeles Times*, September 13, 2000.
Frank J. Murray	"Innocents on Death Row," *Insight on the News*, November 22, 1999.
Ronald J. Tabak	"Racial Discrimination in Implementing the Death Penalty," *Human Rights*, Summer 1999.
James Q. Wilson	"What Death-Penalty Errors?" *New York Times*, July 10, 2000.

For Further Discussion

Chapter 1

1. The author of the first viewpoint argues that for criminals who "have no expectations beyond the Grave," only capital punishment will serve as a deterrent. In Cesare Beccaria's view, why is long-term imprisonment a more effective deterrent to criminals than death? Which author do you find more persuasive, and why?
2. Horace Greeley contends that capital punishment "weakens the natural horror of bloodshed" and teaches disregard for human life. How does John Stuart Mill counter this argument? In Mill's opinion, what does the death penalty teach about human life?
3. Robert E. Crowe maintains that criminals often commit murder in the course of robberies "on the theory that dead men can make no identifications." In Clarence Darrow's opinion, why do burglars often kill their victims? What does Darrow think is the cause of criminal behavior? How does his view contrast with Crowe's?

Chapter 2

1. After reading the viewpoints in this chapter, which do you believe is a more just sentence for the crime of murder: the death penalty or life in prison without parole? Defend your answer with evidence from the text.
2. John Kavanaugh contends that the state devalues human life when it executes murderers to declare that killing is wrong. Michael D. Bradbury disagrees, arguing that the death penalty affirms life's sacredness by enabling the state to kill those who take life. Kavanaugh is a columnist for a Catholic magazine; Bradbury is a district attorney. Does knowing these authors' backgrounds influence your assessment of their arguments? Why or why not?
3. Peter Berger argues that the death penalty is intolerable because it is a form of cruel and unusual punishment. Michael Scaljon maintains that execution methods generally treat murderers more humanely than the killers treated their victims. In your opinion, which author offers the more compelling argument for or against the death penalty? Explain your answer.

Chapter 3

1. Compare the graphs presented in Jay Johansen's viewpoint with the one included in the viewpoint by Christine Notis and Ed-

ward Hunter. Which of these graphs offers the strongest support for the respective authors' arguments about the death penalty and deterrence? Explain.

2. Wesley Lowe maintains that capital punishment must be consistently applied for it to be effective as a deterrent. Paul H. Rosenberg contends that the death penalty actually increases the rate of violent crime. What evidence does each author present to support his conclusion? Whose argument is more convincing? Why?
3. William Tucker asserts that the death penalty effectively deters felony murders, while Steven E. Landsburg argues that a high number of convictions is a more effective deterrent than executions. In each viewpoint, try to find two supporting arguments that you personally agree with. Why do you agree with them?

Chapter 4

1. Eugene H. Methvin contends that wrongful executions are highly unlikely. Moreover, he believes that the death penalty should be retained even if there is a small possibility of innocent people being executed. What objections do Clarence Page and Richard Cohen have to the ideas articulated by Methvin? Which viewpoint do you agree with, and why?
2. Mark Costanzo and the Friends Committee on National Legislation maintain that the death penalty is applied disproportionately to blacks, particularly when their victims are white. How does Dudley Sharp explain this phenomenon? Do you find his explanation convincing? Why or why not?
3. According to Rodney Ellis and Joseph Fiorenza, why should mentally retarded defendants be exempt from the death penalty? How do you think Cathleen C. Herasimchuk would respond to their arguments? Defend your answer using examples from the text.

Organizations to Contact

The editors have compiled the following list of organizations concerned with the issues debated in this book. The descriptions are derived from materials provided by the organizations. All have publications or information available for interested readers. The list was compiled on the date of publication of the present volume; the information provided here may change. Be aware that many organizations take several weeks or longer to respond to inquiries, so allow as much time as possible.

American Civil Liberties Union (ACLU)
Capital Punishment Project
125 Broad St., 18th Fl., New York, NY 10004
(212) 549-2500 • fax: (212) 549-2646
website: www.aclu.org

The project is dedicated to abolishing the death penalty. The ACLU believes that capital punishment violates the Constitution's ban on cruel and unusual punishment as well as the requirements of due process and equal protection under the law. It publishes and distributes numerous books and pamphlets, including *The Case Against the Death Penalty* and *Frequently Asked Questions Concerning the Writ of Habeas Corpus and the Death Penalty*.

Amnesty International USA (AI)
322 Eighth Ave., New York, NY 10001
(212) 807-8400 • fax: (212) 627-1451
website: www.amnesty-usa.org

Amnesty International is an independent worldwide movement working impartially for the release of all prisoners of conscience, fair and prompt trials for political prisoners, and an end to torture and executions. AI is funded by donations from its members and supporters throughout the world. AI has published several books and reports, including *Fatal Flaws: Innocence and the Death Penalty*.

Canadian Coalition Against the Death Penalty (CCADP)
PO Box 38104, 550 Eglinton Ave. W, Toronto, ON M5N 3A8 Canada
(416) 693-9112 • fax: (416) 686-1630
e-mail: ccadp@home.com • website: www.ccadp.org

CCADP is a not-for-profit international human rights organization dedicated to educating the public on alternatives to the death penalty worldwide and to providing emotional and practical support to death row inmates, their families, and the families of murder victims. The coalition releases pamphlets and periodic press releases, and its website includes a student resource center providing research information on capital punishment.

Death Penalty Focus of California
74 New Montgomery, Suite 250, San Francisco, CA 94105
(415) 243-0143 • fax: (415) 243-0994
e-mail: info@deathpenalty.org • website: www.deathpenalty.org

Death Penalty Focus of California is a nonprofit organization dedicated to the abolition of capital punishment through grassroots organization, research, and the dissemination of information about the death penalty and its alternatives. It publishes the quarterly newsletter *The Sentry*.

Death Penalty Information Center (DPIC)
1606 20th St. NW, 2nd Fl., Washington, DC 20009
(202) 347-2531
website: www.essential.org/dpic

DPIC conducts research into public opinion on the death penalty. The center believes capital punishment is discriminatory and excessively costly, and that it may result in the execution of innocent persons. It publishes numerous reports, such as *Millions Misspent: What Politicians Don't Say About the High Costs of the Death Penalty*, *Innocence and the Death Penalty: Assessing the Danger of Mistaken Executions*, and *With Justice for Few: The Growing Crisis in Death Penalty Representation*.

Justice Fellowship (JF)
PO Box 16069, Washington, DC 20041-6069
(703) 904-7312 • fax: (703) 478-9679
website: www.justicefellowship.org

This Christian organization bases its work for reform of the justice system on the concept of victim-offender reconciliation. It does not take a position on the death penalty, but it publishes the pamphlet *Capital Punishment: A Call to Dialogue*.

Justice for All (JFA)
PO Box 55159, Houston, TX 77255
(713) 935-9300 • fax: (713) 935-9301
e-mail: jfanet@msn.com • website: www.jfa.net

Justice for All is a not-for-profit criminal justice reform organization that supports the death penalty. Its activities include circulating online petitions to keep violent offenders from being paroled early and publishing the monthly newsletter *The Voice of Justice*.

Justice Now

PO Box 62132, North Charleston, SC 29419-2132
e-mail: ranlerch@geocities.com
website: www.geocities.com/CapitolHill/8169

This organization supports the death penalty as a solution to the problems of crime and overcrowded prisons in the United States. It maintains information resources, which are available to the public, consisting of books, pamphlets, periodicals, newspaper clippings, and bibliographies about serial killers, death row prisoners, executions, prisons, and courts.

Lamp of Hope Project

PO Box 305, League City, TX 77574-0305
e-mail: ksebung@c-com.net • website: www.lampofhope.org

The project was established and is run primarily by Texas death row inmates. It works for victim-offender reconciliation and for the protection of the civil rights of prisoners, particularly the right of habeas corpus appeal. It publishes and distributes the periodic *Texas Death Row Journal.*

Lincoln Institute for Research and Education

1001 Connecticut Ave. NW, Washington, DC 20036
(202) 223-5112

The institute is a conservative think tank that studies public policy issues affecting the lives of black Americans, including the issue of the death penalty, which it favors. It publishes the quarterly *Lincoln Review*.

National Coalition to Abolish the Death Penalty (NCADP)

1436 U St. NW, Suite 104, Washington, DC 20009
(202) 387-3890 • fax: (202) 387-5590
e-mail: info@ncadp • website: www.ncadp.org

The National Coalition to Abolish the Death Penalty is a collection of more than 115 groups working together to stop executions in the United States. The organization compiles statistics on the death penalty. To further its goal, the coalition publishes *Legislative Action to Abolish the Death Penalty*, information packets, pamphlets, and research materials.

National Criminal Justice Reference Service (NCJRS)
U.S. Department of Justice
PO Box 6000, Rockville, MD 20849-6000
(301) 519-5500 • (800) 851-3420
e-mail: askncjrs@ncjrs.org • website: www.ncjrs.org

The National Criminal Justice Reference Service is one of the most extensive sources of information on criminal and juvenile justice in the world. For a nominal fee, this clearinghouse provides topical searches and reading lists on many areas of criminal justice, including the death penalty. It publishes an annual report on capital punishment.

Bibliography of Books

Mumia Abu-Jamal — *All Things Censored*. New York: Seven Stories Press, 2000.

James T. Acker, Robert M. Bohm, and Charles S. Lanier, eds. — *America's Experiment with Capital Punishment: Reflections on the Past, Present, and Future of the Ultimate Penal Sanction*. Durham, NC: Carolina Academic Press, 1998.

Amnesty International — *On the Wrong Side of History: Children and the Death Penalty in the USA*. New York: Amnesty International USA, 1998.

Jan Arriens, ed. — *Welcome to Hell: Letters and Writings from Death Row*. Boston: Northeastern University Press, 1997.

Hugo Adam Bedau, ed. — *The Death Penalty in America*. New York: Oxford University Press, 1998.

Walter Berns — *For Capital Punishment*. Lanham, MD: University Press of America, 2000.

John D. Bessler — *Death in the Dark: Midnight Executions in America*. Boston: Northeastern University Press, 1997.

Robert M. Bohm — *Deathquest: An Introduction to the Theory and Practice of Capital Punishment in the United States*. Cincinnati: Anderson Publishing, 1999.

Craig Brandon — *The Electric Chair: An Unnatural American History*. Jefferson, NC: McFarland, 1999.

Scott Christianson — *Condemned: Inside the Sing Sing Death House*. New York: New York University Press, 2000.

Mark Costanzo — *Just Revenge: Costs and Consequences of the Death Penalty*. New York: St. Martin's Press, 1997.

David Crump and George Jacobs — *A Capital Case in America: How Today's Justice System Handles Death Penalty Cases, From Crime Scene to Ultimate Execution of Sentence*. Durham, NC: Carolina Academic Press, 2000.

Shirley Dicks — *Death Row: Interviews with Inmates, Their Families and Opponents of Capital Punishment*. New York: iUniverse.com, 2001.

Herbert W. Haines — *Against Capital Punishment: The Anti–Death Penalty Movement in America: 1972–1994*. New York: Oxford University Press, 1999.

Jesse Jackson — *Legal Lynching: Racism, Injustice, and the Death Penalty*. New York: Marlowe, 1996.

Robert Johnson — *Death Work: A Study of the Modern Execution Process*. Belmont, CA: Wadsworth, 1997.

Katya Kazin — *Finding Life on Death Row: Profiles of Six Inmates*. Boston: Northeastern University Press, 1999.

David Lester — *The Death Penalty: Issues and Answers*. Springfield, IL: Charles C. Thomas, 1998.

Robert Jay Lifton and Greg Mitchell — *Who Owns Death? Capital Punishment, the American Conscience, and the End of Executions*. New York: William Morrow, 2000.

Dan Malone and Howard Swindle — *America's Condemned: Death Row Inmates in Their Own Words*. Kansas City, MO: Andrews McMeel, 1999.

James J. Megivern — *The Death Penalty: An Historical and Theological Survey*. Mahwah, NJ: Paulist Press, 1997.

Michael A. Mello and David von Drehle — *Dead Wrong: A Death Row Lawyer Speaks Out Against Capital Punishment*. Madison: University of Wisconsin Press, 1998.

Lane Nelson and Burk Foster, eds. — *Death Watch: A Death Penalty Anthology*. Upper Saddle River, NJ: Prentice Hall, 2001.

Kathleen A. O'Shea — *Women and the Death Penalty in the United States, 1900–1998*. Westport, CT: Praeger, 1999.

Louis J. Palmer Jr. — *The Death Penalty: An American Citizen's Guide to Understanding Federal and State Laws*. Jefferson, NC: McFarland, 1998.

Louis J. Palmer Jr. — *Encyclopedia of Capital Punishment in the United States*. Jefferson, NC: McFarland, 2001.

Louis P. Pojman and Jeffrey Reiman — *The Death Penalty: For and Against*. Lanham, MD: Rowman & Littlefield, 1998.

Helen Prejean — *Dead Man Walking: An Eyewitness Account of the Death Penalty in the United States*. New York: Random House, 1993.

Mei Ling Rein, Nancy R. Jacobs, and Mark A. Siegel, eds. — *Capital Punishment: Cruel and Unusual*. Dallas: Information Plus, 2000.

Austin Sarat, ed. — *The Killing State: Capital Punishment in Law, Politics, and Culture*. New York: Oxford University Press, 1998.

Lloyd Steffen — *Executing Justice: The Moral Meaning of the Death Penalty*. Cleveland: Pilgrim Press, 1999.

Ted R. Weiland — *Capital Punishment: Deterrent or Catalyst*. Eugene, OR: Far Horizons Press, 2000.

Robert V. Wolf and Austin Sarat, eds. — *Capital Punishment: Crime, Justice, and Punishment*. Broomall, PA: Chelsea House, 1997.

Index

DISCARDED